INTERMEDIATE DOWNHILL SKIING
BALANCE IN MOTION

GARY POSEKIAN
AND
BOB O'CONNOR

MASTERS PRESS

A Division of Howard W. Sams & Co.

Published by Masters Press
A Division of Howard W. Sams & Company
2647 Waterfront Pkwy E. Dr, Suite 100, Indianapolis, IN 46214

© 1996 Gary Posekian and Bob O'Connor
All rights reserved. Published 1996

Printed in the United States of America.

No part of this publication may be reproduced, stored in a retrieval system, or transmitted, in any form or by any means, electronic, mechanical, photocopying, recording, or otherwise, without the prior permission of Masters Press.

96 97 98 99 00 01   10 9 8 7 6 5 4 3 2 1

Posekian, Gary, 1955-
    Intermediate downhill skiing / Gary Posekian and Bob O'Connor.
      p.   cm.
    ISBN 1-57028-100-9
    1. Downhill skiing.   I. O'Connor, Robert, 1932- . II. Title.
GV854.P573   1996   96-43654
796.93'5--dc20   CIP

Contents

PREFACE 1
INTRODUCTION 5
1. BUYING AND TRYING EQUIPMENT 11
   What Makes A Ski Ski? 14
   High Performance Racing Skis 16
   High Performance Recreational Skis 18
   Ski Boots 19
   Racing Boots 22
2. BALANCE IN MOTION — STARTING WITH
   THE FEET 27
3. IT'S ALL IN THE FEET 35
4. THE MID-BODY CONTROL OF BALANCE 53
5. THE UPPER BODY'S CONTROL 63
6. BASE CARE AND WAXING 79
   Choosing The Right Wax 81
   Tools And Accessories For Base Preparation
   And Waxing 82
   Safety Precautions 84
   Preparing The Base Structure Of Your Skis 87
   Wax Hardness And Color Coding 89
   Care Of The Edges 91
   For Racers And Advanced Skiers 92
   Swix Alpine Waxes 92
7. CONDITIONING 97
   Conditioning For Cardiorespiratory Endurance 97
   Developing Muscular Endurance 100
   Increasing Your Strength 101
   Becoming More Flexible 115
   Training For Agility And Balance 116

Acknowledgements

We would like to thank Gerhard Pagels and Brad Peatross for their expert photography. Thanks also goes to our ever tolerant and competent editors Holly Kondras and Heather Lowhorn, and to Tom Bast, the chief honcho at Masters Press who had faith in the project from the beginning. Thanks to Christy Pierce for the cover design.

The people at the Swix in Lillihammer, particularly Harald Bjerke, gave us great information on the latest in waxing techniques and products.

Our models for the conditioning chapter were Christian and Sollaug F. Arnessen. Christian owns the Kom I Form training center — Oslo's finest.

Dedication

To my wife and kids, thanks for all your patience.
— Gary

To Kari, my favorite person and consumate ski buddy.
— Bob

PREFACE

There are many inherent pleasures with downhill skiing that make the sport quite addicting. First and foremost are the grandeur of the mountains and the winter environment. There is nothing quite so magnificent as freshly fallen snow sparkling under a bright, winter sun. The excitement of waking to snow laden trees under deep, blue skies and knowing that it's going to be one of those days on the mountain continues to be one of the great experiences of skiing. The exhilaration of being in the mountains with all the spectacular views and vistas, the camaraderie of family and friends, and that ability to "get away from it all" make skiing one of the most popular modes of winter recreation.

Many varied sensations that make up the sport: the feeling of floating almost weightless through light, fluffy powder snow; the rush and excitement of ripping a high speed, arcing turn across a smooth, freshly groomed run; and that incredible boost you get from a fluid, controlled blast through the moguls. And the best part of all this (and the reason you really need to buy this book) is that the more skilled you become, the more access you acquire to the incredible variety skiing offers. You don't have to be an Olympic medalist to have fun skiing. There is, however, a big chunk of mountain out there, and wouldn't it be great to be able to ski most of it comfortably? If nothing else, you would be getting more return from your lift ticket investment!

But if you ask us, the most meaningful reason to ski is the opportunity it provides to explore, challenge, and extend your personal limits. Let's face it; no matter what level we're talking about, skiing is a physical and mental challenge. Unlike other sports, with skiing your opponent is a mountain. Not a stupid little ball that you'd like to send to the moon with your set of clubs. Not your cheating friend, who calls every ball you hit "out." Yes, my friends, in skiing the mountain just sits there and makes no apologies for your weaknesses. Nor does it congratulate you on your merits. So you may as well learn to go with it.

INTERMEDIATE DOWNHILL SKIING
BALANCE IN MOTION

Intermediate Downhill Skiing

The coauthor, having figured out "how the heck they do that," enjoys the fruits of his labor. Contrary to popular belief, you don't have to be born on skis to ski this way. Perseverance, dedication and practice of the basics can enable anyone to experience the thrill of skiing.

INTRODUCTION

If I had a nickel for every time a skier came to me for a ski lesson and said, "I just want to know the secret," I'd be a millionaire. We skiers all want to know the one thing — that elusive 'secret' — that would make us ski gods and goddesses. Having learned to ski as an adult rather than having grown up on skis makes it easy for me to relate to the person who just wants to know 'the secret'. I recall vivid memories of watching ski heroes on Mammoth Mountain, California, glide through snow conditions I would struggle with, grunting and groaning down the mountain. "How do they do that?" I would ask myself in frustration.

I had the same number of feet, arms, and legs as they did. They appeared to be no stronger nor were they particularly brilliant athletes. They weren't even that good looking! To my somewhat naive perceptions, however, my ski heroes were capable of superhuman feats on skis. It wasn't that they were flying off cliffs or doing aerial somersaults or anything like that. No, what was really impressive was the almost nonchalant manner in which they would blast through diabolical skiing situations.

In deep, heavy, wind crusted snow conditions that would leave me sweating and coughing up blood, they would float along as though they were on a packed run. At speeds I don't feel comfortable driving my car, they would skirt through moguls like deer bounding through the woods. I can even remember once watching in amazement as two of my ski heroes carried on a conversation while blasting down one of the Dropout chutes at Mammoth. "How do they do that?"

Convinced that these people had obviously found the elusive 'secret' of skiing and were unwilling to share it with anyone else, it was time to search alone for the "secret." Was it their physical condition? I lifted weights, I rode a bike, I hiked, I ran, I jumped and rolled, I ate right, I lost weight, I felt like a million bucks. And my skiing still stunk.

Well, maybe "stunk" is a bit harsh. I actually did get marginally better — in the crud and deep snow, I stopped coughing up blood. But those same magicians continued to amaze me with the ease they displayed in tough skiing situations. I went back to the drawing board. I read books, I lifted more weights, I ran farther, I jumped higher, etc., etc. And on a particularly bright, sunny spring day, I stood aside one of the more grueling runs down the backside of Mammoth Mountain, and watched my ski heroes slither through the moguls like water running down a creek. "For crying out loud, HOW THE HELL DO THEY DO THAT?!!"

I don't want to give the impression skiing can't be enjoyed unless you're blasting through the moguls or cruising through the deep powder, because it can. However, I have always felt that any recreational activity is more fun if you know what you're doing. And when you get to the level where you go beyond simply participating, to the level of performing at your recreation, you're hooked. I mean, isn't golf more enjoyable now that you can really send the ball as opposed to those days when you'd swing for a home run and produce a bunt? Didn't tennis become a passion for you when you consistently hit the ball over the net? Isn't bowling a lot more fun when,.... well, let's forget bowling.

It really boils down to the fact that learning and progressing with anything is fun. Performing a sport with skill and finesse is fun. Meeting and overcoming challenges in sport is not only fun, it's character building. When I had my first successful blast through the powder, that's when skiing became a passion. Yet on any given weekend at any ski area in the world, skiers are content to slide around aimlessly, just getting to the bottom of the hill. If they only knew just how much fun this sport can be.

But forget about the fun for a second. You're plopping down a lot of cash for that lift ticket; wouldn't you like to ski your money's worth of mountain? You see, with skiing, getting better doesn't just enable you to hit the ball harder or with more accuracy to beat your opponent. With skiing, as you get better, your playing field gets bigger! The fun factor goes up exponentially when you can venture off the beaten path. It becomes an adventure that you just can't get enough of.

When I teach people to ski, I relate skiing in some way to sports my students may have participated in. Actually, when you think about it, skiing is quite similar to other sports. We have a playing field (the mountain), a play thing (the skis and boots), and the athlete (you). Let's look at each ingredient just a bit closer.

First of all, skiing, as with other sports, is performed on a playing field. Basketball is played on a basketball court. Baseball is played on a baseball field. Golf is played on a golf course. Skiing is played on a mountain. The best skiers have an intuitive, playful sense for their playing field and their relationship to it. Great skiers know how to flow with the lay of the land in the same way that an accomplished golfer approaches a shot for the green. They intuitively manage the boundaries of speed and control with the agility of a professional running back weaving down the sidelines of a football field.

Next we have the apparatus, or plaything, that is used to play the sport. Those of you who played basketball in your youth will remember the bond you formed with your basketball. It became a part of you and you would dribble it everywhere you went. On your way to the school bus, the local drug store, and on the neighborhood basketball courts for the afternoon two-on-two. Spinning it on your finger, dribbling it around your body and through your legs, tossing it up in the air. Handling a basketball became as easy and natural as walking.

Great skiers also possess this sense of ease with their skis. Their feet are as accustomed to maneuvering and directing a pair of skis down the mountain. Good skiers also move and balance over their feet in a way that actually allows the equipment to do most of the work. As you will discover in the chapter on equipment, skis are designed to turn. The trick is in knowing what to do to make them go where you want to go.

This leads us to you, the player. Given the apparatus and playing field, the best athletes perform their art with such precision and ease it almost appears magical. Think of Michael Jordan and the way he dances around opposing basketball players. Totally free of the preoccupation with technique, athletes at this level simply act and react, and as a result, their performance appears effortless. How many times have you watched good skiers dance down a steep, bumpy run, thinking how easy that run looks. You then attempt the same run and flounder hopelessly, wondering, "How do they DO that?!!"

As frustrating as it may be, I do think it's educational to take a close look at what great athletes do that make them great, and try to do what they do.

Why reinvent the wheel? Why go through the time and trouble trying to figure out how to do it when someone else already has?

Now, as many of you athletes and coaches may already know, the best athletes in any sport are those who have mastered that sport's applied fundamentals. You know the basics. The best athletes are not magicians who have some secret trick they do that nobody else knows about. They are simply the product of natural talent and a lot of disciplined, concentrated effort toward mastering their sport's fundamentals. Top athletes work for hours — tennis players on their stroke mechanics; baseball players in the batting cage; golfers driving balls just working on their swing; they're all refining the basic movements of their sport. Well folks, with skiing, it's no different.

The best skiers are masters of the basic movements of skiing. There are variations in their style based on individual strengths and weaknesses, but the basic movements are the same. And there's another little trick that great skiers know; skis are designed to turn! That's right, skis will turn if the skier knows how to use them. All it takes is the ability to tip and press the ski's edge into the snow and balance over the skis as they turn across the hill. Great skiers know this. They all tip the ski on it's edge, press it into the snow and direct it with their feet and legs in the direction they want to go. It's how the ski itself is designed to be used. Great skiers ski in a manner which allows the equipment to do most of the work. To do anything else would be akin to using a pair of pliers to hammer in a nail.

And because of the equipment, skiing down a mountain is incredibly simple. Just swing 'em left and right and don't fall; that's all there is to it. Sounds simple enough, however, performing it is another matter. You see, if all we ever skied on were slopes as smooth as billiard tables, with consistent pitches and fall lines, skiing would be almost automatic. We would simply perform the same movements over and over again, with no variation in our timing or coordination. We would never have to worry about varying the shape of our turns to regulate our speed or avoid obstacles, and we would never lose our balance because there's nothing to throw us off. Skiing would be easy; a piece of cake; BORING!!!

Heck, one of the reasons we ski is to be free of the routine and monotony of everyday life. The beauty of skiing is the diversity it offers; the addiction of skiing becomes dealing effectively with that diversity. That's what keeps us coming back for more. Those runs through the moguls or deep snow where, for just a couple of turns, you feel it. Everything just flows and what once was a challenge is now a source of pure joy. This is the addiction of skiing.

INTRODUCTION

The beauty and diversity of all-mountain skiing.

It's what hooked me. I was grunting and groaning, struggling with some snow condition or slope when all of a sudden, CLICK!! Things came together and off I went.

For those of us who didn't grow up on skis but have that burning ambition to be great skiers — there are some shortcuts to greatness. It is possible to find the way to skilled skiing quickly. In the process of mastering these basics you can make breakthroughs in your skiing. In my own case, I became a very intent student of the sport, and the process of learning to ski better also taught me how to be a better ski teacher. I would basically field test my teaching methods on myself. Learning what worked and what didn't for me as a skier greatly enhanced my teaching.

And so it is with this spirit that this book has been written. We can share with you some of the concepts and approaches that have helped many intermediates to advance quickly in their skiing skills. And as has been already pointed out, you don't have to have been born on skis to learn these basic concepts. The intent of this book is to bring that experience to you and, hopefully, allow you to maximize your learning and speed your progress as a skier. It is written with simplicity and clarity, and the exercises and concepts will enable you to make breakthroughs in your skiing.

We won't waste your time with a lot of dialogue and a million different things to think about. We're going to keep it simple and focus on a few key points that you are going to get very good at. The interesting thing about skiing is that if you develop one good habit, such as a well balanced stance, five bad habits go away.

So read on, my friends. This book will not confuse you. In fact, throughout the reading, you will be asking yourself if this is all there really is to skiing. Well, we're here to say that, yes, skiing is a simple sport, and our hope is that this book communicates that idea. It will take some disciplined effort on your part in practicing the exercises presented, but your skiing will definitely improve quickly. And on that bright, sunny spring day, as you effortlessly dance through the moguls and hear the people who are watching you say, "HOW DOES HE DO THAT?!!" you can tell them.

CHAPTER 1
BUYING AND TRYING EQUIPMENT

Before we get deeply into any discussion of technique, we need to talk about modern ski equipment, and the effect good equipment can have on your skiing. Now, relax; I'm not going to try to sell you anything. But if you're still sliding around on those old wooden Head Biflexibles, with a pair of lace-up boots assaulting your feet, you owe it to yourself to take a spin on the modern skis and boots today. You won't believe the difference.

More than ever before, it can be truthfully stated that the skis and boots of today will definitely make you a better skier. The new "shaped", or "super sidecut" skis, will handle a tremendous variety of terrain and snow conditions. These skis, with their deep sidecut and shorter design length, are making previous models obsolete. The boots, with softer flexing plastic composition and various canting and stance adjustments, are now more versatile and adaptable for a wider range of skiers. Even bindings are contributing to ski performance with various systems designed to enhance the flex and dampening characteristics of today's skis.

It's interesting to see how the ski industry's marketing and design philosophies have evolved through the years. Ten or fifteen years ago, the manufacturers produced 'racing' skis, and 'recreational' skis. If you skied with speed and aggressive technique, you skied on 'racing' skis, and everything else was done on 'recreational' skis. The racing skis were stiff and demanding, and were exciting (or challenging, depending on your outlook) to ski. They would grip like a bear on smooth, hard snow but get 'em off the beaten path and into ungroomed snow and they were like riding a Brahma bull.

On the other hand, the recreational skis were easy and forgiving to ski, but lacked the performance when the snow became hard or icy. With softer overall flex patterns, the recreational skis performed well at slow to moderate speeds and softer snow conditions, but became unstable at speed and in firm packed snow conditions.

In about the same time frame, recreational skiing was beginning to be challenged by other leisure activities; golf, tennis, bicycle riding, snowboarding; the skiing boom days of the 70's and early 80's were a thing of the past. The ski industry had to get smarter. So they took a look at what was going on out there in the real world of leisure sport — oversized tennis racquets, lightweight golf clubs using sophisticated materials, snowboarders carving up the mountain showing turns that skiers only dreamed of making. The leisure industry wisely began making itself more accessible to their consumer. Ski equipment manufacturers went to the drawing board with this influence.

The evolution that ensued has lead to the equipment being produced today. Ski boots, for example, transmit the skier's movements with precision and accuracy. Yet the modern plastics being used make these boots much more forgiving when compared to some of the higher performance models of the past. Today's performance ski boots actually feel softer flexing. This characteristic allows the boot to dampen the impact of bumps and rough snow conditions without disrupting the skier's balance. In the past, a softer flexing boot would yield under the higher lateral forces of advanced skiers. Today's boots, however, effectively isolate fore/aft flex from lateral flex, producing a boot which is supple in the rough, yet powerful and stable laterally. Indeed, the ski boots of today are a far cry from the man-eating plastic monsters of years ago. Interestingly, this design revolution didn't necessarily come out of nowhere. Much of the sophistication of boot design has been in response to the evolution of ski design.

More so than ski boots, ski design has gone through quite a metamorphosis from the stiff, heavy planks of twenty years ago to the lightweight cruisers of today. The modern "super sidecut" or "shaped" geometry that is revolutionizing modern ski design has drastically improved the performance and versatility of today's skis. Compared to traditional ski construction, these new skis are lighter, easier to turn, and have a much greater range of performance in varying terrain and snow conditions. Now, more than ever before, ski manufacturers are producing skis that consumers can purchase as their all purpose, all mountain ski. Gone are the days of purchasing a pair of skis for the moguls, one pair for the deep stuff, and a pair for hard snow.

It isn't just coincidence that ski technique has gone through a similar evo-

BUYING AND TRYING EQUIPMENT

Tip the ski, press the ski, twist the ski, and the ski does the rest. This has been a property of ski design for over two decades now, but today's skis do it better than ever!

lution over the years. As ski and boot design evolved through the years, the world's best skiers intuitively discovered how to fully exploit the performance of the newer designs. Skis got lighter, softer, yet generated tremendous edge holding properties. With less effort required to manage the skis, the best skiers began skiing with more precision and more efficient application of their strength and power — and their technique became the model on which ski teaching based it's methodology. So as you can see, equipment design has played a significant role in the evolution of ski technique.

But enough of this! What you want is some advice on what equipment to buy. Well, the best way to make an educated purchase is to educate yourself. Don't leave everything to the ski shop salesperson. You should go into a ski retailer with a basic knowledge of what is available, and more importantly — knowing what you want. Do you want to be a racer, or are you happy just cruisin' around on the smooth groomed runs? Are you going to jump off cliffs and ski down elevator shafts? Or are you more interested in floating through moguls and deep snow with more grace and ease than you ever imagined? Whatever your passion, there's stuff that will take you there.

WHAT MAKES A SKI SKI?

OK, so let's talk about skis. What makes 'em work? Why do they go left and right? And what makes some skis go left and right better than others? For the answer to these and other perplexing questions, we'll need to talk about some of the fundamentals of ski design. Let's start out with the element of sidecut.

You'll notice that the ski is shaped somewhat like an hourglass, being narrow in the mid-section and wider at the tip and tail. If you took this ski and set it on its edge on a flat surface, you would see the tip and tail contact the surface but there would be some air beneath the middle. Now, if you began to press against the middle of this ski, while on its edge, the ski would bend until the entire length of the ski contacted the flat surface. Now imagine this ski, tipped on its edge and bent into the snow, scribing an arc as it travels over the snow's surface. This, in oversimplified terms, is basically how skis are designed to turn. Take a ski, tip it on its edge, press on it, and point it where you want it to go, and you go there. Of course, there are a few variables out there that will complicate things, but we'll deal more with all of that later.

This is the area of ski design that is creating all the excitement today. Generally speaking, a ski with a deeper, more exaggerated sidecut (in other words, narrower in the middle and wider at the tip and tail), will make a tighter turn radius with less effort than a ski with a more shallow sidecut. This is where contemporary skis differ radically from skis manufactured as recently as three to five years ago. The sidecut of today's skis are much deeper.

This is one reason these skis are so responsive and possess such a powerful edge grip on hard snow. However, it's important to know, as we discuss the various design aspects of skis, that it is the blend of these characteristics that will influence a skis' performance, and not any one particular element.

The property of a ski that allows it to bend and flex along its length is known as the flex characteristics of a ski. Ski flex characteristics vary according to the type of ski and the intended performance category. As we said in our discussion of sidecut, the ski must be on its edge and bent into the snow for its sidecut to be effective, so you can see the interrelationship between flex and sidecut. Generally speaking, (and this is a gross generality) softer flexing skis tend to be easier to turn at slower speeds, while stiffer skis provide stability at speed and strong edge grip on hard snow. A softer flexing ski also tends to perform better in deep snow and moguls than would a stiff flexing ski.

By placing varying amounts and types of materials along the length of a ski, ski manufacturers can stiffen or soften different sections of the ski. This is known as the flex distribution of a ski, and it has a significant influence on how a ski will perform. When a particular section of a ski is softer flexing, that section will bend and dig into the snow deeper than other sections of the ski. For example, a softer flexing tip of the ski will bend deeper than the mid and aft sections. The net result of this is that the ski will start turns quite easily as the tip bends and deflects the ski across the snow. Once again, it's a trade-off as that soft tip will tend to become skittery at high speeds.

Another type of flex that will affect ski performance is torsional flex. Torsional flex simply means how easily the ski twists about its length. (This means the amount of movement along the line from the middle of the tip to the middle of the tail.) Again, torsional flex must be considered in conjunction with other characteristics, but usually a ski with stiff torsional flex will perform well on hard snow surfaces. On the other hand, the stiffer torsion tends to make a ski somewhat unforgiving in rough and bumpy snow conditions. Rather than flexing and conforming to the terrain, torsionally stiff skis tend to skip and bounce across uneven terrain. Conversely, torsionally soft skis are more manageable in the rough and in softer, inconsistent snow conditions, but skid and become unstable on hard snow surfaces.

The weight of a ski has a significant influence on its performance. Obviously, a lighter weight ski will feel more maneuverable and responsive than a heavier ski. However, while a lighter ski will feel quick and easy to turn at slower speeds, it can sometimes also become skittery and quite nervous at higher speeds. And as you might have guessed, heavier skis may feel sluggish at slow speeds and quick turns, but provide quiet stability at high speeds and rough snow conditions.

There are many other design aspects of alpine skis that we really don't need to go into. The characteristics we've discussed here are the ones with which you should familiarize yourself. It will help in making an educated decision about what type of ski to buy. Don't worry, you can be confident that whatever you decide to invest in, you will be getting a quality product. There are very few lousy skis being produced nowadays. There is a great deal of variation in the feel of these skis, however, and it is strongly suggested that you embark on a serious "try before you buy" program.

Most ski shops offer a demo program where you can take skis for a trial spin. It's great fun and you can learn a lot about how different types of skis perform under different terrain and snow conditions. Moreover, if there's not much snow and you're skipping across the rocks and dirt, with sparks flying off your skis' edges like a roman candle on the Fourth of July; WHO CARES! They're not your skis! (Just kidding ski shops...heh heh!!)

As has been said before, there are several categories of performance for which skis are designed. It will help to know something about them. Remember that all skis are designed to excel in a particular performance environment, with some doing some things better and others doing other things better. Primarily, we'll discuss the characteristics of high performance racing skis and high performance recreational skis. Within these categories, just about everyone from an intermediate to Superman can find what they're looking for. Even within these categories there's quite a range of performance, with various skis — each having their own niche. Once again, the "try before you buy" program is the suggested approach.

HIGH PERFORMANCE RACING SKIS

Just like the category implies, skis in this group are normally at their best on a race course, where the snow is hard packed to icy, and the speeds are fairly high. This category represents the top of the performance ladder, and these skis are best suited to advanced skiers. Racing skis need to be stable at higher speeds on hard snow. They must also be capable of tremendous edge grip in order to hold a clean, arcing track on the race course. In ski racing, skidding through the turn is like putting the brakes on. Consequently, racing skis tend to be on the stiffer side of the flex spectrum, both torsionally and longitudinally. They are also relatively narrow, particularly underfoot, with a more exaggerated sidecut. Today's competition skis, however, are quite different from the racing skis of the past. Some of the older designs achieved their edge hold and stability with brutally stiff torsional and longitudinal flex characteristics, and they were a handful to manage in varying snow conditions.

I remember a pair of limited edition, race stock, turbocharged, fuel injected skis I had about ten years ago. They were magic on hard, icy snow. They held a line like they were on a rail. However, my first spin on those beasts in deep, cut up junk snow was death-defying. Because they were so stiff, they deflected off every piece of snow they came in contact with, and just getting to the bottom of the hill alive was an accomplishment. By comparison, today's racing skis are softer flexing overall, yet maintain and even surpass the edge holding traits of older designs. Additionally, because they are softer in flex, they tend to be more versatile and easier to ski for all-mountain type skiing.

There are several categories of race skis, and their construction varies according to the event they are designed for. Generally speaking, you should consider slalom and giant slalom type skis. They are the most practical alternative for general purpose skiing, unless you plan on skiing at 70 mph.

Slalom skis are designed for quick turns on hard packed snow surfaces. In ski racing, the slalom races are held on steep, icy hills with gates set closer together. Consequently, speeds are moderate, and the priority is making a quick, clean arc past the gate. To accomplish this, slalom skis are quite stiff torsionally, and have a softer flexing tip to make it easier to start the turn. They get progressively stiffer toward the tail since slalom technique involves finishing the turn with some pressure on the tail of the ski. They are also quite narrow in width under the foot.

The sidecut on slalom skis has gone through quite a change in just the past couple of seasons. Once again, at the risk of sounding repetitive, you should take a test spin on these boards before buying. While some of these slalom skis will slice through the ice like butter, with their stiff tails and narrow overall width they will sink like a submarine in deep snow. I discovered this last season when I went cartwheeling through some of the famous Mammoth Mountain deep powder while trying a friend's pair of prototype slalom skis.

Giant slalom (GS) skis, on the other hand, make a great all-around ski. Their flex pattern is normally more balanced, meaning they flex more evenly from tip to tail. They also have materials that tend to make them ski quieter on the snow, and have less of that tendency to skip around in varying snow conditions. They are made for skiing at higher speeds, as giant slalom races have gates that are set more openly spaced. We're still talking hard snow, and GS skis have great edge hold, with deeper sidecuts than past models, so they can still make a quick turn. Personally, I prefer skiing on GS skis most of the time because they are so versatile and forgiving to ski. Don't get me wrong here, some slalom skis are quite well rounded and their quick, lively nature can be a blast in the bumps and on steeper hills. Different strokes for different folks, you know. Whatever your choice may be, you can rest assured the ski you purchase today will outperform anything you've ever skied on in the past.

There are other competition skis on the market that are suited for the "speed events" in ski racing, namely Super Giant Slalom (Super G) skis and Downhill skis. As said before, however, if you plan on turning, forget these puppies. They are made for high speed ski racing, and are really not much fun at recreational skiing speeds, unless your idea of fun is crashing through the moguls like a runaway laundry truck.

HIGH PERFORMANCE RECREATIONAL SKIS

If you ask me, this is where all the excitement in skiing is today. In this category you will find skis with sidecuts so radical it's amazing. These are the "super sidecut" or "shaped" skis you will be hearing about in the years to come. These skis are more versatile, more fun, easier, more forgiving in a wider range of conditions than anything else I've been on.

As we mentioned before, some racing skis are just too high strung to be really enjoyable in deep snow, moguls, and steeper terrain. Modern shaped skis overcome this by combining the stability and edge grip of racing skis with the ease of turning of shorter skis.

The shaped skis still have torsional rigidity, so they will grip on all but the iciest snow surfaces, but where they really shine is in the real skiing world of inconsistent, varying snow and terrain conditions: deep inconsistent snow, moguls, steeper terrain, and rough cut up snow. This is the domain of today's high performance recreational skis, and these skis can definitely help you ski better in these conditions. Once again, there is a broad range of personality in this group, with some skis' performance leaning toward moguls and deep snow, while others are more suited to recreational ski racing and hard snow performance. In general, however, these skis are more versatile than all-out racing skis, and you can be confident that anything produced by one of the major manufacturers will perform for you.

Now, there are a lot more categories of skis out there that we really don't need to talk about. It can be quite overwhelming to go shopping for equipment these days, as the manufacturers are producing such a variety of skis. Don't sweat it! First of all, give some serious thought to exactly what you want, and what type of skiing you really enjoy. If you like spending a lot of time in the moguls and deeper snow, choose accordingly. Look for a slightly softer overall flex for this type of skiing. If you prefer moderate speed cruising on mostly groomed slopes, look for firm flex with stronger torsional strength to give stability and edge hold. The point is, spend most of your efforts deciding what kind of skiing you want to do, roughly how many days you plan on doing it, and where you plan on doing it. Then you can leave the rest to the ski shop salesperson.

It is helpful to educate yourself as far as what the manufacturers are offering and how they perform. Here the ski magazines are quite useful, if you know how to read them. The magazines perform on-slope tests of most of the top brands early in the season. My advice is to read them — very closely. Read all the reports and read them again and again. Try to get a feel for which skis the testers raved about, and which they thought were just OK. You really have to read between the lines, because there are few poor performing skis out there. Spend enough time reading them so you can get a feel for what worked and what didn't. Narrow your choices to maybe two or three different pairs, then take them for a ride.

Pay close attention to your very first impression of the skis you're trying. This is a basic principle of testing skis, as with more time on new skis your movement patterns will adjust. It is also important to try skis in as wide a variety of conditions as you can find. You don't want a pair of skis that limit you to one part of the mountain.

SKI BOOTS

Well, if you thought buying skis was complicated, wait until you try shopping for boots! There are so many to choose from, and so many that work so well, that the process of buying ski boots can be quite difficult. Once again, however, the manufacturers are producing such a variety of fit and performance offerings that somewhere out there is a boot that will work for you.

Do your best to persevere through the shopping process and make a very well thought out purchase, because your ski boots are your most important piece of equipment. If they don't fit comfortably, or they aren't the correct stiffness for your skill level, the fun factor goes down considerably with your skiing. Consequently, ski boot design is much more complicated than ski design, as the aspects of fit, comfort and stance vary greatly from skier to skier.

As mentioned earlier, ski boot design has come a long way since the days of stiff, uncomfortable leg-eating plastic casts of a decade past. Modern plastics combined with contemporary design theories have produced ski boots that can perform and fit comfortably. However, having a basic knowledge of some of the aspects of ski boot design will definitely help you know what to look for when you begin your shopping venture. Quite obviously, a ski boot must fit comfortably for it to perform to its potential, but there's a lot more to boot fitting than just having comfortable dawgies.

Your ski boots are the foundation for balancing over your skis. They must support you and allow you to move and react in balance. They are also the transmission device through which you will apply turning forces to your skis.. For this to happen, not only must they fit comfortably on your feet, they must also align accurately with your entire lower body structure from the pelvis all the way down to the soles of your feet. If the ski boots are aligned, or canted incorrectly, it will be difficult to accurately adjust the edge angle of the skis, and your skiing will be a constant struggle for balance. Take it from me, the difference between skiing with the right fit and the wrong fit is night and day. So, let's talk more specifically about a good 'fit'.

Technically, a good fit requires the correct applications of biomechanics — the application of physics or mechanics to the body. It is essential to know some of the "whys" of fit and design before we get into the "whats" of boot styles. It is important to know a bit about how the boot interfaces with the skier so you know why and how to get a good fit.

Remember that skiing is balance. Maybe they should call it "alpine balancing." Anyway, you'll hear it said here about a thousand times, but it's true. And when we talk about balance, we're talking specifically about balance in motion. We're not standing like a robot on top of those sticks, we're movin', baby. Now, if we were skiing in heaven, we would be skiing in perfect balance all the time, skis going where we wanted them to, when we want them to, roaring through mogul fields with total composure. (Maybe in heaven, there are no moguls!)

BUYING AND TRYING EQUIPMENT

Skiing is balance in motion. Proper fitting, well-aligned ski boots can make or break your balancing efforts on skis.

Here in the real world, however, we are not in perfect balance all the time. In fact, sometimes we're in perfect imbalance. Because of this, skiing down a hill is as much a series of balance adjustments as it is balancing movements. Now keep in mind your skis are your point of contact with Mother Earth. Hence, the accuracy and precision with which the skis move over the snow will have a huge influence on the accuracy and precision of your balance. If the skis are tipped too high on their edges because your boots are overcanted, the edges will grab the snow erratically and you lose your balance. If the skis are not tipped high enough on their edges because the boot is undercanted or too soft, the edges will slide out from underneath you and again you lose your balance.

As you can see, the crucial role the ski boots play in this whole scenario is that they transmit the lateral movements from your lower body into edging movements to the skis. When you roll your knee inside to get the ski to turn, the boot transmits that movement and tips the ski up on its edge. If there is an alignment problem between your boot and your lower leg, the ski will always get tipped too high or too low on the edge, and you'll never really be in good balance. This is why boot manufacturers are making their boots with adjustable cuffs that can be aligned to anyone's lower leg. This, however, resolves only part of the problem, as correct alignment really starts at the soles of the feet. The point is that a good fitting boot is a bit more encompassing than just being able to wiggle your toes.

As is the case with skis, ski boots are targeted for various performance categories, and they pretty much follow the same format, with boots being produced for racing, for general high performance skiing, and for your basic recreational comfy, cozy ski boots.

Let's talk primarily about racing boots and high performance recreational boots. Between these two categories, just about anyone from an intermediate to an expert level skier can find what they're looking for. Besides, these are definitely the most fun to talk about.

RACING BOOTS

Remember our discussion of racing skis and who they're appropriate for? Well, the same concept applies even more strongly to racing ski boots. These shoes are primarily designed for the demands of race courses that are set on steep hills with hard, icy snow conditions. As such, these babies are stiff, stiff, stiff! These boots are not going to feel like bedroom slippers on your feet, and they are not the easiest to walk around in or get in and out of. They are designed to perform, and that's just what they do.

Actually, some of these designs have been around for over fifteen years, coming out every year in some newfangled rendition, with various bells and whistles to suit the current marketing trend. The basic bare bones nature of these boots, however, reflects the fact that these boots are no frills racing machines, and they offer no apologies for your pain or discomfort. I don't mean to scare you here, but believe me, buying a boot that's too stiff and rigid is not going to speed your learning progress. You can get away with getting skis that are beyond your skill level and still have a great time skiing on them. However, when it comes to boots, shop carefully and thoroughly. Demo, demo, demo! And of course, read the magazines.

If you are an advanced to expert skier, racing boots can make your skis do things you never thought possible. Because they are constructed of stiffer plastics, the response of these boots is amazing. Consequently, many of today's racing boots demand an expert's reactions and precision of movement, as any lateral movement of the legs is transmitted directly to the skis' edges. The design of these boots brings them a bit higher up the leg than recreational ski boots, and they can generate incredible edge holding forces on hard snow. They also tend to be very stiff flexing to the rear, which enables top skiers to accurately apply strong pressure to the tails of the skis. The stiff rearward flex also aids in balance recoveries in rough, bumpy terrain.

The forward flex of racing boots has been softened over the past few years, mostly due to the fact that today's skis are so much easier to manage. However, when compared to general purpose/all terrain ski boots, racing boots are still quite stiff in forward flex. As a result, some of the stiffer models can be a handful in the bumps and in varying snow conditions for all but the best skiers. At any rate, if you're primarily interested in slammin 'the boo' (running gates) and your youthful, steely legs and knees don't grind and crackle when you bend them, a pair of these fire-breathing racing boots may be the call.

Frankly speaking, however, unless you plan on spending a lot of time on the race course, you'll do much better opting for some of the detuned racing models. Their softer flexing plastic and lower cuff height won't punish your mistakes as severely, and skiing in bumps and softer snow will be much easier. You'll find these models categorized by a number of different names, but they are generally referred to as all-terrain or all-mountain ski boots. In most cases, the manufacturers simply inject a softer plastic composition into the same mold the racing boot comes out of, producing a boot that approaches racing boots in lateral response and power, but with softer fore/aft flex making the boot easier to balance with.

Speaking from personal experience, softer boots make all-mountain skiing much easier. If you've been banging around for the past few years on a pair of stiff flexing race boots, you owe it to yourself to try something softer. I'll never forget trying a pair of softer flexing boots after having made the U.S. Demonstration Team. I'd been egotistically skiing on a pair of super stiff race stock boots and this particular sponsor wanted me to try their newer release. Being the eternal pessimist and always resistant to change, I went into the testing process basically having decided I was going to hate these softer mush buckets. By the end of the day, I was skiing through situations and conditions with more speed and confidence than I had ever been able to muster with my "bat out of hell" racing boots.

The reason? Well, going back to the sermon on balance, remember we said your skis are your point of contact with ground zero. The more smoothly we can direct the skis through the turn, the more solid and stable our balance over the skis will be. Now, as we said, the racing boots are very responsive and will hold that ski's edge in smooth, hard snow like a vise. However, sometimes we don't want a vise-grip hold on some snow conditions. In fact, soft and inconsistent snows will punish you for that vise-grip hold and cause your skis to go to parts unknown. This is precisely what I found out when I tried these softer flexing boots.

In big, ugly moguls with a few inches of new snow over rock-hard frozen slush, the skis were much easier to manage. In wind and sun crusted snow conditions, the skis tracked smoothly and predictably through the turn, as opposed to that dreaded diving of the tips I'd been accustomed to having to adjust to. Rather than deflecting and skipping off every little inconsistency, my skis floated over and through the death cookies and I remained stable and in control.

I was convinced; I went softer and haven't looked back since. I'm not saying soft boots are for everyone, but if you're struggling in your skiing, especially with ungroomed snow conditions, just try going softer. You may like what you feel.

Something to keep in mind when trying ski boots is that it will take longer to adjust to an unfamiliar boot than it will with skis. Your movement patterns, particularly if you're an advanced skier, will have become grooved to the specifics of the boot you're comfortable in. Because of this, the try before you buy program with boots is a bit more involved. Make sure you give yourself ample time to adjust to the stance of a different boot before making any judgments. With boots, your first impression may not be the most accurate. Also, as with skis, be sure to test boots in as varied snow and terrain conditions as you can find. Look for conditions that challenge you and see if the boots you're trying make those conditions easier to ski. If they do, you've got yourself a pair of ski boots!

I want to reiterate the fact that there are few, if any, bad skis or boots out there these days. Whatever you decide to buy, it's money well spent. Just make sure it works for you before you make an investment. Also realize that your ski boots will probably need some customizing to get them to accurately fit your foot and lower leg. I can't overstress the importance of a knowledgeable boot fitter in this area. You could spend five hundred bucks on a pair of the best boots on the market, and if they're improperly aligned to your leg and ankle structure, you won't be able to buy a turn. Talk to some of the locals at your ski area and find out who's doing good boot fitting and get yourself checked out.

Well, we've talked enough of ski tech for now. The main point is just how much better today's equipment really is. Don't get me wrong, you still have to turn 'em, but it's so much easier and so much more fun than the equipment of just five years ago. If you ski at least five to ten days per year, and you want to get more out of your investment in a lift ticket, just give the stuff a try. You are guaranteed to feel the difference. Now... let's make some turns!!

Intermediate Downhill Skiing

Fundamental Balance: Ankles and knees flexed, hands in front and out to the side for stability, vision directed straight ahead, this smilin' dude is ready for action.

CHAPTER 2
BALANCE IN MOTION — STARTING WITH THE FEET

Okay, folks; we've got you equipped with all the high tech stuff. Now, there are no excuses — you gotta ski!! As I've mentioned previously, today's equipment is designed to make this sport easy, but it won't do it on its own. You have to tell them what to do. You have to balance with them to guide them where you want to go. You have to coordinate your movements so the skis can do their job. It's all up to you, you, YOU, the skier.

If there's one underlying theme that I would like you to get from this book, it is that you need to allow the equipment to do most of the work for you. And to get the most out of the equipment, you must learn to balance and move through specific movement patterns which enable the skis to do their thing. Have you ever heard the term 'sweet spot' applied to skiing? Well, it applies. Skiing is one of those balance and movement oriented sports that has a sweet spot. In tennis, the racquet has a sweet spot that drives the ball with power and accuracy. Top tennis players focus on contacting the ball with the sweet spot of the racquet in the same manner golfers seek the sweet spot of the golf club. When you think about it, almost any sporting activity has a sweet spot. Top athletes realize this and learn to seek the sweet spot of their sport with consistency and accuracy.

In skiing, the skis have a 'sweet spot' that, when a smooth application of pressure is applied, drives the skis with unbelievable power through just about any kind of snow or terrain in their path. Now, the sweet spot varies from ski to ski; some skis possess a smaller sweet spot than others, making them a bit more demanding. But once you find that sweet spot of a particular ski, make it your home base position from which you do all of your skiing. Become as comfortable and familiar with it as if you were dribbling your basketball around the neighborhood. Learn to feel for it and seek it in the same way you would feel for that wonderful 'thunk!' of a baseball landing in the pocket of your baseball glove.

Without a doubt, learning to be at home with the 'sweet spot' of your particular sport is one of the keys to removing the barriers of high performance. As I've observed through years of teaching skiing, getting a skier to stand in the 'sweet spot' of a pair of skis enables them to make the breakthrough they seek. Extraneous movements begin to disappear, and they begin to experience the excitement and exhilaration of skiing in balance. Gravity becomes an ally rather than an adversary, and terrain that was once unmanageable is now a source of playful joy.

Now, as I said, the sweet spot does vary slightly from ski to ski, but there is a zone that you can key into that should become your home base position for your skiing. Quite simply, this zone exists along the lengths of the soles of your feet, and to really improve your skiing, you must become at home balancing over this zone of your feet. This means adjusting everything, your arms and hands, your hips, and your head, such that the result is your mass being supported by the lengths of your feet.

To really tune into said sweet spot, you should become sensitive to the soles of your feet. You should be anyway — after all, you're on them all day. Every day as you walk to and fro, you unknowingly pass through the proverbial sweet spot of skiing and you probably didn't even know it. Becoming sensitive to the soles of your feet is critical to performance skiing because your feet can tell you where your balance is at any given moment. But enough lecture, let's get physical!

Get up out of that chair and assume the skiing position; the one you see all the cool guys using. As you stand there with your knees well flexed, your hands held loosely in front of you, tune into the soles of your feet, young grasshopper. Try to sense where your body weight is being supported, and experiment with the effect moving your body forward and backward has on your balance zone. You will feel it pass from the balls of your feet through the balance zone under your arches to the heels of your feet as you rock fore and aft, my son. Believe it or not, you are taking the first steps toward developing an entirely new awareness of your balance; it's that simple!

Now, I only wish skiing was as physically easy as standing there with your knees bent in the middle of your living room. Things get a bit more complicated as you begin to move down the mountain, and suddenly the earth begins to pass swiftly beneath your feet. This is what makes skiing so unique. Balance, as it relates to skiing, involves being able to maintain your contact with your balance zone, as you move down the mountain. It's a gliding type of balance, as opposed to balancing over a fixed platform, such as just standing there over your feet.

It boils down to the fact that in skiing, the balance applied is balance in motion, or dynamic balance. Basically, all efforts to balance can be thought of as dynamic, since balancing is a constant series of adjustments. For example, get back out of your sofa for a minute. Assume the position we talked about before, with your knees well flexed, weight balanced over the length of both feet. Now, I want you to lift one foot and attempt to maintain balance. You'll notice that even as you stand there, relatively motionless over your foot, you are continually making minute adjustments with your hands and arms, through your waist and lower body. So even though you're standing basically still, there are subtle movements your body performs to maintain balance. These subtle balance adjustments are also critical to performance skiing, and we will discuss them in depth a bit later. Right now, we want to look closer at how to be at home with home base.

As I said before, becoming sensitive to the soles of your feet is very important because it enables you to feel what balance adjustments are necessary. A balanced stance means your weight is supported by the lengths of both of your feet. An out of balance stance would be with your weight supported by the heels of your feet. We want to position ourselves such that our body weight is distributed along the length of the skis. This is important because it enables you to control every centimeter of those babies. Imbalance places you over a small segment of the skis' length, causing that portion of the ski to grip the snow, while the rest of the ski wanders over the snow. This is what is often responsible for problems like crossing the ski tips, or not being able to start or finish turns effectively. Skis will not perform as designed if you are not properly balanced over them.

Now as we work up from the feet, other body segments are positioned and aligned such that you are carrying your weight over home base. Let's move up to the ankles. One of my fellow ski instructors at Mammoth, Mike 'Fitz' Fitzmaurice, likes to start his beginner lessons with an entertaining diatribe about stance on skis. "Folks," he says, "I would like to clear up some of the misinformation you may have heard in some of your previous ski lessons, and I'll start with your stance. How many times have you been told to bend your knees while skiing?.... Well, I'm not going to ask you to bend your

INTERMEDIATE DOWNHILL SKIING

"Home Base" shown from the side. With practice, correct body alignment and positioning becomes a good habit. Alpine skiing then becomes...

...effortless!

knees, I'm going to ask you to bend your ANKLES!"

The effervescent Fitz is right on! Bending the ankles is essential to developing a good stance. Look at a pair of ski boots from a side view, and you'll notice the upper half of the boots are angled forward. Your ankles should be flexed to conform to this alignment of your ski boots. It should be enough that when you are standing in your skiing stance, there is a firm pressure against your shins from the tongue of your boots. This you should feel the entire time your are skiing.

You would think that with all that stiff plastic and buckles around your lower leg, it would be impossible to get any flex or movement out of your ankle. Not so. Remember our little exercise where we stood on one leg? Let's do it again, but this time I want you to close your eyes and put your hands on your hips. As you'll find out, this is not easy. However, take a few stabs at it, and you'll begin to notice a few things. The one sensation I want you to key into is how your ankle is constantly adjusting laterally to keep you balanced. These small adjustments are possible and essential inside ski boots as well, and later we'll discuss how to become more sensitive through your ankles to enhance good balance.

At this point, if all we did was to balance the weight over the lengths of the feet and bend our ankles, we would wind up with our nose against the tips of the skis. So, let's adjust the knees and hips over the feet and ankles so that our hips are plumb over our feet.

Take a few minutes to put your ski boots on and stand in front of a mirror (my wife loves it when I parade around the house in my ski boots, slamming them into the walls, furniture, etc.). As you stand there imagining the fresh breeze in your face, the people riding the chairlift admiring your flawless technique, observe the relationship of your hips to your feet. This relationship is critical to good balance, and we should spend a few minutes to get a good understanding of it. Try to imagine a string with a weight attached to it, dropping straight down from your hip bone. Now rock your hips forward and backward over your feet. As you do so watch where the string line falls alongside of your foot. Now positon your hips over your feet such that the stringline falls just ahead of the arch of your foot. Presto! You've found home base.

At the risk of sounding oversimplified, this is your home base position from which you will do your best skiing. Keeping your hips and mid-section aligned over your feet in this zone is the secret to skiing in all conditions at any speed. If you learn nothing else from this book but this, your skiing will improve. But let's not stop there. For, just above the mid-section exists yet another body segment that, if used properly, will make balancing over your feet much easier. I'm talking about your hands and arms.

As we develop balance capacities throughout our physical development, we learn to use the hands and arms to stabilize ourselves, especially in situations where balance is challenged. Observe the way gymnasts carry their hands as they perform routines on the balance beam. The hands instinctively adjust and move for balance and stability. In skiing, the hands are as essential to good balance as any other body segment.

Let's once again stand on one foot for a few minutes (you probably didn't realize just how physical reading this book was going to be). Now close your eyes, and move your hands out away from your body to stabilize and settle your balance. You'll notice as you move them farther away from your body, your balance will become more stable. This is a principle you can apply to skiing. The position in which you carry your hands has a tremendous influence on your ability to stay balanced over the home base. For skiing, we want them out away from the body, and carried in front of the hips. You don't want to be skiing around like a mummy, with your hands held stiffly in place, but rather loosely carried in a zone in front of your body, just within your peripheral vision.

This brings us to the last body segment I want you to become sensitive to, your eyes. Your vision and your ability to visually scan the terrain will have a tremendous influence on your skiing. To understand just how important your vision is, try skiing with your eyes closed sometime. It is incredibly difficult! Your vision and how you use it is probably the most neglected aspect of performance skiing, and improving your ability to use it will definitely improve your skiing.

You have probably noticed that we have been discussing skiing in terms of what to do with various segments of the body, and this is where we'll go from here. I am going to tell you how to coordinate the various body segments so that the input you give to your skis is effective. Then we can let the skis do the rest. Specifically, the body segments, or zones we will key into will be; the lower body — i.e., your feet, ankles, knees, and hips; the mid body — your abdomen, waist, and lower back; and the upper body — your hands, arms, shoulders, and head. I'm going to tell you how to move and coordinate these three zones to achieve your goal of skiing like a hero. We will key into sensations and feelings and I will tell you what to do both on and off the snow to develop finesse of movement with these body zones.

You will, however, have to take some responsibility for your development. In our discussion of the various body segments and how to use them, I'll present an exercise designed to develop an awareness. You should practice the exercise, on and off the snow, and learn how to integrate it and use it to enhance your skiing. Try to become a student of this wonderful sport, and come up with some exercises on your own that you will improve with. I can tell you there is nothing more fun than learning and progressing.

CHAPTER 3
IT'S ALL IN THE FEET

Let's begin our learning process with the lower body. After all, this is your connection to the skis, and your lower body executes the movements needed to direct the skis down the mountain. The role of your mid and upper body is simply to balance over these movements in your lower body. We will talk primarily of tipping movements, and twisting movements of the lower body for skiing. So let's start right down there at ground zero with your feet.

Skiing starts at the feet, pure and simple. The skis are attached to your feet, and are primarily guided and controlled by your feet. The great Jean-Claude Killy used to speak of something he would call 'intelligence of the feet.' This is one of the essential ingredients of good skiing, and you should devote some effort toward developing it. When skis are running over the snow surface, they are constantly being knocked around by all the inconsistency of the snow surface. It's your feet that can pilot those skis through and around these obstacles, and the more sensitive and aware you are through your feet, the more precisely you can guide the skis where you want them to go.

To get a better understanding of this, simply lift your ski off the snow and twist it left and right with your foot. This is an oversimplified example of what's happening on snow as you twist and turn your feet down the mountain. The ski tips are basically an extension of your feet. Wherever you point your feet, your ski tips follow. As such, it becomes critical to your development as a ski maestro to develop the 'intelligence of your feet'. Which basically means let's teach our stupid feet what to do with those six foot planks attached to them. This is something you really have to discipline yourself to develop, unless you have grown up on skis and have that innate sense through your feet. (In which case, why are you reading this book?)

Intermediate Downhill Skiing

Your skis are an extension of your feet. Developing your "foot awareness" and ability to direct your skis with your feet will improve your skiing.
This is a static exercise you can do on the side of the hill to improve your foot's awareness of the ski.

Generally speaking, Americans are not particularly 'foot-sensitive' as a society. By this I mean we engage in primarily upper body oriented sporting activities (although in recent years, with the increasing popularity of in-line skating, soccer, and other sports, this seems to be changing). The sports we grow up playing are focused on power, strength, and coordination through the mid and upper body. In baseball, we swung the bat using our arms, shoulders, and through our trunk. We played basketball, dribbling and shooting the ball with our hands and arms. And in football, just move the bloody ball down the field; anybody gets in your way, just knock 'em down!! The primary role the lower body plays in most domestic sports is to get us where we want to go, be it straight ahead or sideways, fast or slow.

In skiing, however, the lower body, and particularly the feet, are the primary directional controllers of where the skis are going at any given time. I'm sure we've all experienced that dreaded tip-crossing scenario a few times. Nine times out of ten, this is caused by poor coordination between the feet. Simply put, the left foot going right and the right foot going left! In alpine skiing the feet aren't so much a means of propulsion as much as they are precise steering devices, guiding the skis along the desired path. The feet also serve as your primary source of feedback telling you where your balance is being carried. Becoming sensitive to the soles of your feet and where you feel your weight being carried over them is essential to good skiing.

If the skis go where the feet point them, and we want to be in control of the skis, we need to learn to act and react through our feet. As I said before, developing sensitivity and dexterity through your feet can take some time and discipline, but it can be done. It is most important that you realize you can develop this both on and off your skis. If you really want to develop foot sensitivity, there are some exercises you can do on and off the snow that will enhance your foot awareness and sensitivity. Let's start on dryland.

Keep in mind that the feet serve as our contact with ground zero, providing constant feedback as to where we are positioned over them. We know that our 'home base' balance zone for skiing is when our weight is carried along the entire length of the soles of our feet, so this is what we should feel for. However, this doesn't mean that you should lock up all parts of your body motionless like a robot, in an attempt to stand balanced over your feet.

Quite the contrary, and in fact to develop consistent balance over the soles of your feet, you should experiment with relaxed balancing over and across every square millimeter of your feet. For example, let's get back out of the sofa for a minute or five. Before, we rocked back and forth along the length of the foot soles to feel where the weight was being carried. Let's now take it a step further. Let's get really weird!!

I want you to stand with your knees well bent, and your feet about shoulder width. Holding your hands palms facing down and slightly ahead of you, move from side to side very slowly over your feet. Feel your weight pass slowly from the heel of your left foot to the ball of your left foot. Then slowly from the ball of your left foot to the heel of your right foot, and again to the ball of your right foot. Repeat this pattern over and over, keeping your knees bent deeply. You should feel as though you're moving your mid section in a figure eight pattern over your feet. Notice I didn't say your hips, but your mid-section. You can use your belly button for a focal point.

Now, a few things to keep in mind as you do this exercise. Most importantly, do this exercise very slowly. What we are trying to develop is a connection between what your feet feel and how your body moves to achieve accurate balance. Hence, move very slowly with your mid-section through your figure-eight pattern. Feel the weight pass through every little nerve ending along your foot soles. Try to create a pattern underneath your feet that would leave a figure-eight imprint in the ground. Your weight should pass smoothly from the right edges of the ball of your feet, to the left edges of your heels, then across your heels to the right side, smoothly forward to the left edges of the balls of your feet, and back to the right side of your feet.

This exercise was taught to me by a weirdo friend of mine who was into Tai-Chi. The first time he showed it to me, my laughter made it a bit difficult for me to really tune into the value of the exercise. To humor him, however, I stuck with it for awhile and found the focus on and awareness of my feet really helped my skiing. This exercise should develop a sense of being anchored in good balance over the lengths of the feet. We want to develop the habit of coming back to this zone of balance whenever something throws us out of it.

My personal favorite for off-snow ski training is in-line skating. We will go into in-line skating a bit more in depth in the chapter on dryland training, but I want to mention here that this is another exceptional activity that develops both foot sensitivity and balance awareness. Once again, your ability to balance over a moving platform is being developed. Because your base is only the length of your feet as opposed to two-hundred centimeter skis, the balancing becomes more critical and is confined to a shorter zone. In other words, less room for error.

IT'S ALL IN THE FEET

Turning the feet on the lift...

...and on the snow.

Intermediate Downhill Skiing

As skating has become so popular over the past several years, I've noticed how quickly kids who skate learn skiing. With skating as a background, the skill of gliding balance is already developed. There is no time lost on learning how to balance on a moving platform. Skating kids are ripping on the mountain in no time.

Another dryland activity that develops tremendous foot awareness is soccer. Soccer players are some of my best students. The inherent awareness and dexterity they possess through their feet enables them to learn skiing quite easily. They quickly adapt to the task of handling skis with their feet, and they don't seem to be bothered by things like crossing their tips. So if you don't already play soccer, take it up! Play it with your kids, friends, or whatever. You don't necessarily have to play competitively to reap some of the benefits that will cross over to your skiing, either. Just dribbling the ball around, kicking it back and forth, and passing it around will begin to teach your feet to take responsibility for their actions.

OK, so you get the idea of what we're trying to do with your feet. You should be able to come up with some exercises of your own that will accomplish the goal. Keep in mind that you will learn what to do with your feet quicker if you exercise off snow as well as on snow. So now that you've developed these perceptive tootsies, let's talk about how to use them on your skis. In fact, right off the bat, I'm going to give you a little drill to do the next time you ride the lift. The great thing about this drill is that it directly duplicates the movement pattern with your feet you should develop to make ski turns. It's so simple, it's ridiculous! Just twist your feet left and right; that's all there is to it.

Quite simply, sitting there with your feet dangling over the edge of the lift, simply twist your feet left and right together, trying to keep your skis parallel all the time. Also focus on trying to keep your ski tips and tails about four inches apart as you swing the skis left and right. Try to do this for the length of the chair lift ride. Not only will you be teaching your feet how to direct your skis, you will also be strengthening your lower leg and ankle muscles (not to mention annoying your lift partner!).

Now, when you get off the lift, simply duplicate the same sensations on snow. Try to use the same muscle groups in your ankles and lower legs and apply the torque to the skis in the same manner as you did on the chairlift. Look where you want to go and direct your feet that way. Try not to tip the skis on their edges too much, as this will hamper your efforts to turn your feet. Just keep the skis as flat to the snow as you can while still maintaining your speed, and guide them left and right with your feet and lower leg.

This is a great way to work through your warm-up runs. Rather than just bombing wild down your first few runs in the morning, take it at a moderate speed. Keeping the skis as flat on the snow as you can, concentrate on making your turns by patiently twisting and guiding the ski tips with your feet. Really focus on the last third of the turn where the skis are coming across the fall line, and concentrate your efforts in twisting your feet through this part of the turn. Most skiers during this phase of the turn simply tip the skis on their edges and let the skis take them wherever they're going to go. Not a problem on smooth, groomed, moderately pitched slopes; big problem on bumpy, steep, and varying slopes. Why? Speed, young grasshopper. Speed and control. Generally speaking, it takes longer for the ski to complete a turn by simply tipping and pressing it into the snow. In situations where you want to control your speed, as in steeper pitches, you need to get those sticks across the fall line, NOW!!

This is why it is so important to develop the ability to control the skis' path down the hill with your feet and lower legs. In the words of my friend and former Demo Team member Jerry Warren, "It's the quickest way to get the skis to go from zig to zag."

So, back to the drill we're doing. Let's take it a step further. Once again, keeping the skis flat enough on the snow that it feels as though the skis are sliding sideways, guide the skis across the fall line to the point that they are almost perpendicular to the fall line. As you do this, concentrate on keeping your descent confined to an imaginary corridor of about thirty feet wide. To help you stay inside the corridor, you should keep your vision directed down the hill, as opposed to across the hill. Also, direct your pole plant more or less where your vision is focused. The terrain you should use for this exercise should be smooth, packed snow on a moderately pitched slope.

As you get more comfortable with the task, try to see how many turns you can link before breaking your rhythm. Go for as many turns as your legs can take, and carry your momentum down slopes of varying pitch. It's important to keep turning on slopes that you would normally just go straight down. Doing this will develop sensitivity and teach you how to be precise with your foot-turning movements. By linking hundreds of turns together like this, you will also be developing some efficiency in your movements, as you will instinctively begin to do away with superfluous movements that fatigue you quickly.

You will also learn how to direct the skis through the turn to keep your speed where you want it. Going nonstop down slopes of varying steepness, you'll need to constantly adjust the pace and effort you use to guide the skis to regulate your momentum. On flatter slopes, you should guide the skis through a more direct path down the hill, as opposed to a steeper pitch, where your path is more rounded.

When you feel comfortable directing your skis on smooth slopes, give small moguls a try. Open up the width of your stance and lower your hips a bit more for added stability, and twist and guide the ski tips through the valleys and troughs of the moguls. Keep the speed down — remember you're learning, not competing. Trust me, a few runs spent warming up like this will teach you more about how much skiing is done with your feet than anything else.

I want to reiterate that this is more of a warm-up drill, as opposed to the way you should ski all of the time. We still need to tip the skis on their edges and let the skis do what they are designed to do. However, by keeping the skis flat and guiding the ski tips through the turn arc, your feet are taking command of where the tips are going through the turn. With practice, this awareness can be applied to your skiing in challenging conditions. You will be amazed at how much easier these situations become when your feet do all the thinking.

Another method you can use to develop foot sensitivity is to ski with your boots unbuckled. With the stiff, supportive plastic wrapped tightly around the lower leg, the sensations and feedback from the skis tend to come back to you from the knees up. Because the ankle is supported and locked inside the ski boot, you never really feel the ankle working. Unbuckling the boots, however, removes the support of the upper shaft, and suddenly the foot and ankle become more involved in the whole skiing process.

Be cautious with this exercise as unbuckling the boots can affect the bindings ability to release in a fall. You should ski with your boots unbuckled only on terrain well below your ability. The point here isn't to kill yourself, but to educate your feet, ankles, and knees. You may find the lack of support from the boots unnerving at first, but persevere and you'll develop a whole new awareness of just how much skiing goes on with your feet.

Use some of the natural features on the mountain, particularly moguls, to develop sensitivity and dexterity in your lower body. Using the mogul field as a teaching aid, simply make traverses across them, keeping your ankles

IT'S ALL IN THE FEET

Whether it's long turns to maintain speed, or...

...short turns to control speed, the basic movements remain the same. The key is knowing when and where to vary the timing and coordination of your movements.

Intermediate Downhill Skiing

relaxed and staying loose in your knees and feet. The main goal here should be to keep the skis in contact with the snow as much as possible, while keeping your arms and shoulders as quiet as you can. This is a great balance trainer. It also helps to develop some awareness of where the skis are going and how to control them with your feet. If you're really crazy try it with your boots unbuckled.

You will also find these methods will help your mogul skiing in general. The best mogul skiers are quick, agile athletes who use their feet with beautiful quickness and finesse. They rely less on tipping the skis to control their speed and more on twisting and guiding them with their feet and legs, while keeping the skis a bit flatter on the snow.

Now that we have your feet tuned and ready for action, let's get the rest of the lower body involved in the action. As I said before, we want to be able to use those metal edges to help us go where we want to go, but only just enough that the edges enhance, rather than hinder our turning efforts. This is absolutely essential to good skiing, especially in variable conditions. What we want to develop is an accurate blend of twisting and tipping effort from the feet and legs so the skis go where we want them to. Too many skiers have developed the bad habit of tipping heavily on the edges for control.

I speak from experience, as I have had to make a conscious effort in my own skiing to learn to be softer on the edges, particularly with the new ski designs. My standard M.O. used to be very different. I would stand at the top of the mountain, looking down the steep bumps and firmly packed snow. I was wired from adrenaline overload and too much coffee. The chair lifts passing overhead were full — no empty chairs — it was time for me to excite the masses. I would plant the poles in the snow and push off, accelerating rapidly. Within seconds — speed... more speed... TOO MUCH SPPPEEEEED!!! Crash...bang...slide...humiliation.

Does this scenario sound familiar? I humbly admit I have been there many times. Fact is, often in my skiing career people would stop to watch me skiing down the hill, not so much to admire my technique as waiting to see one of my patented on-snow detonations (nobody asked me how I did that!).

What was happening to me is something I see most skiers experiencing in steeper, tougher skiing situations. Somewhere inside us is a natural instinct to want to lay those edges up high the minute things begin to get away from us. Well, when a ski is tipped high up on its edge, it resists forces that cause it to slide sideways. The ski edges digging into the snow also makes it more difficult to twist and guide the skis with your feet. Consequently, the skis are slower to complete a turn, and they spend more time accelerating in the fall line. Next thing you know...speed...speed...more speed... well, you know the rest. How many times have you been skiing down a run, and before you know it, you're going like crazy and fighting for control? Nine times out of ten, the cause is an improperly timed blending of the tipping and turning efforts in your lower body.

What we need to realize is that there exists an optimum blend of the amount of tip and the amount of twist we apply to the skis for any given terrain and snow condition. If we overdo one or the other, we lose control of the size turn we want to make. If we only twist the skis and never tip them on their edges, the skis will slide sideways across the hill, and we eventually lose control. On the other hand, if we try to turn by only tipping the skis on their edges, the skis rail up and feel as if they are going straight down the hill. Seconds later, your eyes are watering and your face is stretched back as you accelerate to warp drive. This is not how skis are supposed to turn!

Let's begin our understanding of tipping movements with an explanation of why we need to tip the skis on their edges. Yes, it's for control of your skis' speed and direction, but also for stability with your lateral balance. Lateral balance is your balance from side to side. Lacking precision with your tipping movements will make it very difficult to accurately balance laterally over your skis. And if you're out of balance laterally, you're out of balance, period!

How about that dreadful sliding, out of control sensation often felt when skiing on hard snow. You know, where your skis just seem to slide sideways down the hill and you never really feel stable on your feet. This is usually a symptom of not being accurately balanced laterally over the outside ski. Tip the knees into the hill and the shoulders over the feet, and presto — you're back in balance and going where you want to go.

So if refining your sense of lateral movements improves your lateral balance, improving your lateral balance should also improve the precision of your lateral movements, right? Absolutely! In fact, improving your sense of lateral balance will greatly improve your skiing.

How do we find this elusive optimal blend of movements to enable us to ski like a master? Well, to find the right blend of movements, we must first become familiar with them. Since we've spent some time developing some sensitivity in our feet and legs for the twisting effort we want to use, let's now develop the same degree of feel for the tipping movements. Once again, we can expedite the learning process if we first spend time off the snow learning these movement patterns. Balance is balance, whether it be fore and aft, side to side, on or off the snow.

A great example of how involved your lower body is in balancing is to try standing on one foot with your hands on your hips. As you stand there attempting to balance, note how your ankle is constantly adjusting in an effort to keep you stable. Now close your eyes and still try to maintain your balance. You will notice your ankle and knee really getting active in the balancing process. These small movements are important to good skiing, also. Skiing is more or less balancing on one foot over the inside edge of your outside ski. As such, you need to be constantly adjusting in your lower body just as you do in your living room on one foot.

An exceptional dryland exercise that develops good lateral balance is walking on a balance beam. If you're really good, try stringing about 20 feet of rope about a foot or two off the ground between two trees. Personally, I found tightrope walking to be one of the most beneficial dryland exercises for my skiing. I found it gave me a great sense for keeping my stomach right over my feet at all times. When I got on skis, I instinctively went wherever my feet went, and there was no feeling of feet going here and the rest of me going there.

If you decide to try tightrope walking for some ski training, use ski poles for stability at first until you get better. Initially, there will be a tendency for the rope and your lower body to shake and sway from side to side. You'll learn to overcome this with time, and the awareness you will develop in your entire lower body for lateral balance will transfer readily to your skiing.

Do you enjoy running? Well, putting a little twist and turn in your daily running can teach you how to make better ski turns as well. Quite simply, the next time you go for a run, rather than just pounding the pavement for miles on end, put a little zig in your route. Find obstacles to turn around; telephone poles, trees, anything will do. Simulating ski turns in your running will get you feeling the same lateral movements in your lower body used for skiing.

I used to go for runs in the forest all the time. I would run sections around trees as fast as I could, and it helped my skiing. It also made my running much more enjoyable. When I got back on skis, I found myself naturally making the same adjustments in my lower body I had been making all sum-

IT'S ALL IN THE FEET

Good body positioning and alignment allow adaptable skiing. In short turns on steep slopes, the upper body is directed downhill, while the lower body tips and directs the skis.

mer long while running. In particular, my skiing on hard snow got much better, as I learned how to move for balance over the outside ski. It goes without saying that you'll want to do this kind of running early in the morning so no one can see you making a fool of yourself. Now, let's get to some on snow stuff.

One of the best exercises for developing lateral balance and a good feel for the edges is a simple sideslip to an edge set. You may have done them in one of your ski classes at one time. Simply stand on the side of the hill, skis across the fall line, with the edges in the snow. Now roll both knees down the hill and the edges release their grip on the snow. The skis will slide sideways and if you are balanced over them, they will slide directly down the hill. It will help to adjust the skis' direction across the fall line with your feet as you sideslip. If you sense the ski tips drifting down the hill, direct them back up the hill just enough that they are perpendicular to the fall line.

In a sideslip exercise, it's important to be balanced laterally over your feet so you can get the skis to slide sideways. If you have the habit of leaning up the hill, the edges will always be gripping the snow and sliding will be difficult. It's also important to be balanced in the middle of the skis, as any tendency to lean too far forward or back will make it hard to get the skis to sideslip directly down the hill.

Start out by just sideslipping, trying to adjust the skis' edge angle with your ankles and knees so the skis slide sideways smoothly. Make sure you do this in both directions so you don't develop one side better than the other. As you get more comfortably balanced with your sideslipping, it's time to throw in the edge set.

To set the edges from a sideslip, simply tip both knees up the hill. As you do this, make sure you've positioned your upper body over your downhill foot so that ski will bite when you set the edge. If your body positioning is tilted uphill at all, the downhill ski will slide out from under you and you'll lose your balance. As a gauge for body positioning, try to keep an imaginary line drawn across your shoulders which should be parallel to the slope. Doing this will ensure that the torso is balanced over your downhill foot.

At this point, it will help greatly to plant your downhill pole. We'll go into the specifics of good pole use further on, but for right now know that in this exercise a good pole plant is essential. The timing of the plant must be such that the tip of the pole goes in the snow at the same time you set the edges. Try to get a feeling for the pole plant and how it can enhance your body

IT'S ALL IN THE FEET

The next two sequences illustrate the differences in body positioning between turns along the carved (shown here) vs. skidded turn spectrum. Wider, carving-type turns maintain speed and are a blast on smooth slopes...

...However, try them in terrain shown in the next sequence, and I'll visit you in the hospital!

Intermediate Downhill Skiing

positioning. You should eventually feel as though swinging the pole forward brings your shoulders into alignment over your downhill foot.

Now that you know what to do, practice some sideslips on a smooth, moderately pitched slope. Try for crisp edge-sets that stop you at exactly the spot on the snow that you set the edge. If you have the tendency to drift forward or backward after you set the edge, it is a good indication that your balance is either too far forward or too far back. Find the middle of your foot and let snow spray!!

To take this another step further, after you set the edges and release them, begin a turn that will lead to another edge set. To do this, after you set the edges, flatten the skis with your knees and ankles as though you're going to do another sideslip. Keep your upper body rotated directly downhill from you, and stand balanced over your feet. The ski tips will gradually begin to drift downhill, and you can enhance that by adding a little of that twist with your feet. One hint when doing this exercise, and any exercise for that matter, is to keep your feet apart. This will give you stability over the skis, and make it easier to balance with independence from foot to foot.

Now that we're linking edge-sets together, practice the exercise for a few runs. See how aggressively you can set the edge and still get the skis to hold their track. You should perform these linked edge-sets on all kinds of terrain. Smooth, steep slopes are great training grounds, and here you will begin to feel the control that balanced edge use can give you. Realize that when you are on a steep slope, all your movements must be exaggerated. You must roll your knees farther up the hill, and there must be more effort to get your body positioned over your downhill foot at the edge set. And don't forget to keep those feet apart!

I want to reiterate the fact that this is an exercise intended to develop awareness and improve your lateral balance. I don't want you to get the idea that you should ski this way all the time. This exercise will develop your skiing in situations where you need control of your speed and direction, and particularly applies to hard snow skiing. You may feel that a simple sideslip down the hill is a remedial exercise, but in truth it is an excellent drill for learning to balance through your lateral body movements.

With the awareness you are developing in your lower body, experiment with the effect that changing the timing of your movements has on your skis. On smooth slopes, let your speed build and try tipping and pressing the skis into the snow as you start the turn, rather than at the end of the turn.

INTERMEDIATE DOWNHILL SKIING

Here you will feel the skis slice the snow along a more carving, arcing path than in the sideslip/edge set mode.

This basically represents the spectrum between a carved type of turn and one where the skis are guided to an edge set. With awareness and finesse in your lower body, you will learn when and how to blend your movements to optimize the skis' performance in any given snow condition. Smoother packed slopes will call for movements producing a turn leaning toward the carving end of the spectrum. Steeper, bumpy slopes will demand movements to control your speed and direction, tending more toward the skidding side of the spectrum.

The key lies not in developing a carved or skidded type of turn so much as developing the "intelligence" in your lower body to know when and where to effectively blend the movements. Educate your feet and legs so they can do what they need to do, when they need to do it. Now, let's move up to your gut!

CHAPTER 4
THE MID-BODY CONTROL OF BALANCE

When we speak of the mid-body region for skiing, we're talking specifically about the abdomen and lower back, as well as the muscles all the way around your trunk. This zone of your body is directly involved in the balancing process in all sports. It is the center of gravity — the place where your weight is concentrated. It is the link that connects your upper body and lower body and is responsible for positioning and aligning your upper body over your feet. Therefore, it's important that we spend some time learning how to develop strength and power in this region, as well as movement awareness and coordination. No matter how smart your feet and lower body become, if you can't accurately balance and align yourself over your feet through your trunk, your skiing will always be a struggle for balance.

Earlier in the book, we spoke briefly of the involvement of the mid-body in sports. In golf or baseball, a substantial amount of the power generated in the swing comes from the mid-body. The shoulders and arms swing the club or bat, driven and anchored by the power and stability of the trunk. The trunk also provides stability for the upper body of a gymnast performing on a balance beam. Here, the upper body is constantly realigned over the center of the balance beam. This is accomplished through precise movements in the trunk.

Skiing combines the requirements of the twisting power generating movements as well as the subtle aligning movements the trunk is capable of. In many conditions and situations in skiing, the lower body twists against the stability of the trunk, and the two body segments wind up going in opposite directions. In moguls, for example, the lower body and feet pivot and guide the skis through the moguls, while the upper body is kept quiet and aligned down the fall line. Consequently, we need to be flexible through the waist and lower back to enable the considerable amount of twisting movements required.

But without a doubt, the most important role the trunk plays in skiing is keeping the upper body connected to, and moving with the lower body. As the skis drift and slide through a turn, the trunk provides the link between the lower body and upper body, keeping the upper body stable, over and linked to the lower body. No matter how difficult a balance situation may become, as long as the upper body is maintained in alignment over the lower body, you are in balance.

I had this illustrated to me one day when I was walking across an icy parking lot. My mind was wandering, and I walked across a particularly slick patch of ice. Whoosh! Out went my feet from under me to directly in front of me. What happened??!! Quite simply, the relationship between my feet and upper body changed from that of being in alignment, to that of being disconnected. If I had been paying attention to where I was going and had anticipated that the ground would become more slippery, I would have instinctively focused more intently on keeping my shoulders over my feet.

The same thing happens to us when we lose balance on skis. Those are the times when the skis are rolling down the hill for parts unknown, with you the pilot blowing the stop whistle on them. Trees are going by at blinding speed, colors starting to change, with you saying to yourself, "I have become quite disconnected!" For goodness sake, folks, connect yourself. Learn to use your trunk for balance, and you will never become disconnected again! Let's use our approach of teaching ourselves on and off the snow to tune the trunk for balance. Let's start with some exercises that will strengthen your trunk, as well as coordinating and developing some movement awareness through your mid-section.

I'm sure you've done sit-ups until you're sick of them. Well, we're going to do some more, but with a little different twist. Rather than just going up and down until you're ready to vomit, let's make some circles. Start by lying on your back as you would if you were to do regular sit-ups. Now raise up about 6-8 inches off the floor, and move your upper body in a circular motion. Move through a range of motion that maintains tension in your abdominal muscles and try to make nice smooth circles with your upper body. Do about 15 revolutions, then reverse your direction and give me 15 more, YOU SICKLY WIMP!! Just kidding.

This is a great exercise for both strengthening and coordinating your waist all the way across and around the mid-section. You will not only feel the front of your abdomen involved in this exercise, but the sides of your waist as well. Additionally, the task of making circles with your upper body will teach you some movement awareness through your trunk that you will be able to apply in your skiing.

Another exercise that applies well to skiing involves lying down on the floor flat on your back. With your feet and legs held straight out, raise them up so they are more or less perpendicular to your upper body. Now slowly lower them to your left, then raise them and lower them slowly to your right, maintaining that perpendicular relationship between your legs and your upper body. It's important to do this exercise slowly, so as to avoid any potential injury to your lower back. This is an excellent exercise for developing the lateral strength through your trunk that is essential in skiing. It also strengthens muscle groups surrounding the lower spinal column, which will lend stability to this part of your lower back.

If you can get your hands on a stretch cord of some kind, these make a convenient and effective exercise tool for other trunk exercises. A stretch cord is more or less a piece of surgical tubing about eight feet long. By exercising against the resistance of the cord, you can achieve a fairly significant training effect. More importantly, you can exercise through just about any range of motion you would like to. You are not bound to the range of an exercise machine, and because of this, a stretch cord is a great way to condition your mid-section. There's a lot more in the exercise and conditioning chapter. Now let's get on the snow.

Before we get into exactly how we want to align our bodies over the skis, let's talk about why we will be doing what we are going to do. You'll remember that in our talk of equipment, we discussed the fact that the skis turn by tipping, pressing, and twisting or guiding them where we want to go. Well, in order for the press part of this equation to be effective, we need to have the upper body balanced over the outside foot through the turn.

How many times have you attempted to ski the hard, slick snow and had that awful feeling of the skis just sliding sideways down the hill. Typically the reason for this is that your balance is being carried over your uphill (inside), rather than your downhill (outside) foot. What happens then is that your downhill ski, with insufficient pressure applied to it to get it to bite into the snow, simply slides sideways across the snow. Because the ski is sliding down the hill, you never have a stable base to balance over, and the beginning of the next turn becomes a challenge. This whole process becomes self-perpetuating, and your skiing is always a struggle for control.

Intermediate Downhill Skiing

Simple traverses across the hill do wonders for lateral, as well as fore/aft balance.

MID-BODY CONTROL OF BALANCE

The cure for this lies in accurately aligning your upper body over your downhill foot by the proper use of your trunk. This is where you will feel some of the dryland exercises we talked about coming into play. Remember the exercise we did with the stretch cord, flexing and bending sideways through our waist? You will feel that same articulating action as you attempt to balance your shoulders and upper body over your downhill foot. Here's how to do it.

Start with a simple traverse across the hill. As you traverse, tip your knees and ankles uphill just enough that your skis track across the hill on their edges, rather than sliding sideways across the hill. Repeat this traverse in both directions a few times. As you get more comfortable with getting the skis to track across the hill, attempt to perform the traverse while lifting the uphill foot off the snow. It will take a few stabs before you become successful with this one. Balancing on one foot on skis is not easy. You may find it necessary to keep putting the uphill foot back on the snow to avoid falling down. If this happens to you, make some adjustments in your trunk that will tip your shoulders over your downhill foot more.

Learning to balance over your downhill foot is a fundamental skill you need to develop for skiing. With practice, the traverse will become easier for you with one foot off the snow. When this begins to happen, it's time to try making some turns while lifting one foot. Now you will really begin to feel the adjustments necessary to accomplish the task. Quite simply, as you ski through a series of turns, lift your uphill foot off the snow through the turn, and balance over your downhill ski. Here it becomes important to adjust your balance with your trunk to keep your upper body over your downhill foot. Try to feel one side of your waist get shorter while the other side gets longer. The side that gets shorter is the downhill side and will balance your upper body over your downhill foot.

As you complete one turn and are ready to start another one, put your uphill foot back on the snow (making sure not to put it on top of your other foot) and transfer your weight to that foot. As the skis start coming back across the hill towards the last half of the turn, gently lift your uphill foot off the snow and balance over your downhill foot. Now, let me tell you, if you've never done this exercise before, it won't be easy at first. Make sure you practice this on a very smooth, moderately pitched slope. Also make sure to complete every turn so you don't pick up too much speed.

As you do this exercise, you may experience a few problems. I often see people wrestling with the skis sliding sideways down the hill, despite being

Intermediate Downhill Skiing

Skiing with your inside foot off the snow is an excellent balance drill. When you become really good, try this with no poles — however, take care not to step all over yourself!

relatively well aligned over the outside foot. If they are sliding, as opposed to tracking across the hill on their edges, they are less stable, making it more difficult to balance. This is usually caused by not tipping the skis enough on their edges with the knees and ankles. Remember that you can adjust your balance through lateral adjustments of the lower body as well as the upper body. Balancing the upper body over the fine tuning adjustments the lower body makes is the secret of skiing.

If your skis are sliding as you practice this exercise, try going just a bit faster as well as tipping your outside leg to the inside a little more. It is important to combine a bit more tip with a little more speed to keep the skis from railing out and going straight down the hill.

As you get more comfortable and stable with your balance in this exercise, begin to vary the timing of when you lift your uphill foot off the snow. Up to this point you've been lifting it at the end of the turn when the skis are coming across the fall line. Now try lifting it a bit higher in the arc of the turn, more toward the middle of the turn at about the point where the skis are aimed straight down the hill. This will require earlier commitment of your body weight to that outside foot, so adjust your trunk accordingly.

One tip that helps with this is to watch your shadow as you ski down the hill. Try to make sure your shoulders are level with the horizon as the skis enter the fall line and you lift the inside foot. If you have aligned your trunk correctly, your shoulders are level and it's easy to pick the ski up off the snow. If you haven't and your shoulders are tipped to the inside of the turn slightly, you will have difficulty balancing easily over the downhill ski.

By lifting your inside foot earlier in the turn, you are transferring your weight to the outside ski earlier. This will really smooth out the turn and enable the skis to track with more stability across the snow. So, going on the theory that if enough is good, more must be better, let's start lifting the inside foot at the beginning of the turn, at about the point we start to guide the skis down the hill. The movements you should make with your trunk to align yourself are the same, just do them sooner. Transferring your weight this early in the turn allows you to regulate the amount of pressure you apply to the outside ski throughout the remainder of the turn. The main benefit of this is that the skis go through the turn and across the snow much more smoothly. Consequently, they are easier to balance over than skis that are moving erratically and unpredictably.

You can see that through the use of this exercise, you will be developing

Intermediate Downhill Skiing

Groomed trails getting boring? Get creative and learn something! These types of balance drills will greatly improve your skiing — I've got a million of 'em.

MID-BODY CONTROL OF BALANCE

the ability to align yourself for good balance with your trunk. This is essential to good skiing and it will serve you well in variable terrain and snow conditions. Remember, however, that it is an awareness of movement through your trunk that we want to develop so that we can move as we need to. You don't want to develop the habit of transferring your weight at the same point in every turn regardless of the situation. Sometimes the weight transfer should happen later in the turn, sometimes earlier in the turn. Learn to move through your trunk for balance and you will instinctively transfer your weight at the appropriate time for the given situation.

Okay, now that you are skiing around the hill like a flamingo, with one foot off the snow, let's put it back on the snow. Also retain the movement awareness through the trunk to align the upper body over the outside ski through the turn arc, and integrate this back into your free skiing. You should now feel as though you are stable and balanced over the outside ski. You should also feel the outside ski bending and really gripping the snow, giving you a better sense of control in your turns.

After you get bored with this exercise and are looking for a new thrill, try skiing without your ski poles. Talk about a way to get balanced — this is it. Know it or not, when you're skiing with your poles, you'll usually wind up dragging them in the snow as you turn. This gives you some added stability, but also acts as a crutch which allows you to get away with some mistakes. When we ski without the poles, we force ourselves to balance accurately over our feet through our trunk.

This exercise isn't too complicated; just leave your ski poles with a friend or in the locker for a few warm-up runs. Start on something smooth and easy and work up to something mildly diabolical like some small moguls. A few things to keep in mind:

1. Make sure to keep your hands in front of you and spaced fairly wide apart. This will make the adjustments you make in your trunk more effective and give your upper body more stability.

2. Keep your hands in the same horizontal plane — or even tipping downhill as you complete each turn. This will keep your upper body angled over your downhill ski, keeping you in control and smoothing the turn transitions.

3. Spread your feet a bit wider for some stability until you start feeling more comfortable skiing without poles.

4. Make a conscious effort to keep your elbows held out and away from your body. Many people have a bad habit of tucking the elbows right next to the body, in effect mummifying them from the trunk up. This has a tendency to lock up the trunk, significantly inhibiting the fine adjustments required. Hold your elbows as though you've just jumped off a fence and are landing balanced on your feet.

Now, once you get comfortable skiing without your poles, a whole world of exercises are available to you. Ski with your arms crossed. Ski with your hands held on your knees, behind your knees, on your waist, pick your nose while skiing (I do), ski downhill while playing catch with a football — find a left handed friend if you are right handed. Get stupid! Any of these exercises will develop that awareness through the trunk that we're looking for, and they are fun. They have the added benefit of developing some great awareness in your feet — just as taking away the poles put some heightened focus in your mid and lower body. Use the exercises as a way to warm up for a day of skiing, and you'll not only progress and learn something, but your skiing on that day will be at a higher performance level.

Now, let's move up to the upper body.

CHAPTER 5
THE UPPER BODY'S CONTROL

Now that we're talking about the upper body, let's define specifically what we're talking about. When we speak of the upper body in skiing terms, we're talking basically from the arms up. Now, the upper body has a different role in skiing than other sports. For the most part, upper body oriented sports like baseball require power and strength through the chest, arms, and shoulders. With skiing, the upper body should simply remain balanced and quiet allowing the lower body to do its thing. Once again, to remain balanced and stable over your lower body is not to say ski like you have rigor mortis. Remember, balancing is a dynamic process. The adjustments made with your upper body for good balance are minute adjustments, but they exist.

If you have experience in sports involving balance of any kind, you know just how important the arms and hands are in the balancing process. Just try any balance maneuver without using your hands and arms as a balance aid and you'll see. Try walking across a balance beam with your arms crossed. Or attempt that silly one-footed drill I had you doing in your living room with your arms crossed. You'll undoubtedly notice it's a lot easier if your arms are held out away from your body where they can be of use. This concept applies well to skiing, as the position of the arms and the way they're used in the pole plant have a significant effect on your balance.

We will discuss exactly how the upper body should be involved in your skiing. As before, we'll use a few dry land exercises to illustrate the sensations we're after and then relate these sensations to your on-snow skiing. As you will see in this chapter, the movements you'll employ with your upper body for skiing require more dexterity and perception than strength and power.

We should also talk about how important your visual skills are to skiing. When we speak of visual skills, we are talking something a bit different than just having good vision. A great deal of your success as a skier involves the speed and accuracy of your reactions to the conditions in which you're skiing. Put more simply, you see and you react. Being the dynamic sport that skiing is, your visual skills play an important role in your ability to react correctly to the situation. As you will see (no pun intended), good athletic vision will help your performance in all sporting activities.

As we discussed in a previous chapter, sporting activities in this country are primarily upper-body dominant. Our national pastime, baseball, is a prime example. Swing the bat, throw and catch the ball, with your hands and arms. Golf — once again, swing the club with the arms and shoulders and hit the ball. Football, basketball, tennis; watch the ball and hit it, catch it, or throw it with your hands and arms. Then we decide to go skiing and now we're supposed to do something intelligent with our feet!

Well, although the skis are connected to your feet, and your lower body is doing most of the work in skiing, the balancing movements of the hands and arms can have a tremendous effect on your balance — both positively and negatively. The problem most people have is that they don't know *how* to use their arms for balance in skiing.

Most ski teachers feel that wild movements of the hands while skiing reflect some sort of deficiency in the lower body. The common belief is that if there is a weakness in the turning movements of the lower body, the upper compensates and provides the turning power. The net result is that the hands swing around like a matador fighting a bull. Have you ever tried to balance while swinging your hands all over the place? It ain't easy. This is why, as we emphasized in the lower body section, it's important to confine the turning efforts primarily to the lower body. Now the upper body can perform its task of balancing itself over the lower body.

If we place the priority on learning how to balance properly in any given situation, unnecessary body movements begin to disappear. Spend enough time with exercises like walking a balance beam (if you're really good, try a tightrope!), and you will begin to use your hands efficiently for balancing. The key is to focus on maintaining balance using your hands. This may sound somewhat obvious, but you'll notice an improvement in your balance if you concentrate on using your hands.

Balance beam work need not be too technical. A good, sturdy piece of 2 x 4

THE UPPER BODY'S CONTROL

or 4 x 12 about ten feet long will work just fine. Now get on that thing! If you have trouble staying on the beam at first, use a pair of ski poles for stability. Hey, we're not trying to be Nadia Comaneci here! Walk it forward and backward. As you get more comfortable, walk forward and turn around on one foot, then walk for a few steps and spin around again. Concentrate on good posture through your lower back, keeping your knees bent slightly, and most importantly keeping your hands in front of you and out to the side.

Don't tense your muscles in your arms and shoulders. Use only the muscle effort required to keep your arms held up, as any unnecessary tension through your shoulders and neck makes it much harder to sense the balance adjustments you need to make. This is a key principle with balancing — it's sort of a conscious relaxing of specific muscle groups, and it will serve you well in all sports if you get good at it.

One thing about this kind of balance exercise is that some people will be naturally better at it than others. That's why it is best to start off with a wider platform with your balance beam, and use ski poles at first. If you find this too easy and you can comfortably walk the four inch platform, try using a two inch beam. If this is still too easy (you're good), string up a piece of rope about 20 feet long. String it between two buildings. No net! Now we're gettin' down! Seriously you can string up a tightrope, a 3/4 to 1 inch cable or a taut piece of rope on the ground. When you graduate to a skinny little piece of rope, you'll really begin to see just how functional those arms and hands are in the balancing process.

The reason that tightrope or balance beam training is so effective is that the exercise is so difficult, and the feedback so instantaneous, you can't help but learn. You will find yourself so preoccupied with just trying to stay on the stupid rope that you have no room for silly thoughts like 'how's my form.' Consequently, you will learn how to move, think, and react with your upper body for the sake of balance. You'll be amazed at how well this transfers to your skiing. Having learned to move your hands for balance, superfluous movements of your hands and arms will be replaced by clean, purposeful balance adjustments and your skiing will feel effortless. Please remember that it is a very challenging exercise — so avoid getting frustrated. Remember, we're building a skier out of you, not a gymnast!

Actually, you can develop good balancing movements with your upper body in just about any exercise you do that involves balancing over your feet. It will take some conscious effort, but for example — let's say you enjoy hiking. Rather than just lallygagging out there in the woods, put some piz-

INTERMEDIATE DOWNHILL SKIING

zazz into your hike. Jog lightly on the downhills, and as you do, position your hands as you would for skiing or as if you were on that balance beam. You can use the same approach with your running, or your rollerblading. Just keep those elbows away from your body, and keep those hands out and in front. Sure, you'll look like an idiot now, but just think of the turns you'll be making when you get back on snow! Speaking of getting on snow, let's do just that.

You're going to find that time spent on your balance beam really helps you learn new movements and positions with your upper body much quicker. And now that you're on snow, let's try to use the upper body to balance in the same manner you did in your balance training off snow. Position your hands and arms much the same as you do on your balance beam, with them out away from and well in front of your body.

You don't want to get stuck in a position with your hands which makes you ski stiff and posed. This is why it's so important to do your dry land exercises for balance so that you learn how to hold your hands for balance. Now we can concentrate on the other task the upper body must perform — planting that ski pole!

Planting the pole is one of the most misunderstood aspects of ski technique. There is more confusion surrounding the where, when, why, and how to plant the ski poles. Consequently, the pole plant is performed with many interesting variations.

A few years ago, I went through a particularly enlightening learning experience involving my pole plant. I was trying to learn how to ski race at a race camp put on by Rossignol and my coach was George Capaul, who later went on to coach the U.S. Ski Team.

We were training slalom, and George had given a short dissertation of modern slalom technique before we were to begin training. He sent the group back up to the top of the hill for the first run, pulling me aside and telling me in his own inimitable way to make sure I "planted my #@!$%ing ski poles!"

Back at the top of the course, I pushed off aggressively and started to boogie. I'm feelin' good, the edges are holdin', and I'm flyin'! I'm moving my hands and arms all over the place, just like I see the cool guys on television do. I come blasting through the finish and spray the hell out of George, who stands there staring at me. "Great run, eh George??," I thought. Red faced, eyes bulging in rage, he roared in fury, "Posekian, you idiot!!... What the hell are you doing, skiing or ROWING A BOAT!?!" (George was a great motivator). "Give me your poles!" He took them from me and launched them like an Olympic javelin thrower about a hundred yards over the side of the hill. "Now, go back up there and let's see you try to run that course!" I could hear George's laughter from the chair lift.

At the top of the course, I skated into the course and laid into the first turn (without my poles, of course). I survived the first turn, hooked the ski tips on the next gate, and slammed hard. I dusted myself off, put everything back together, started down the course, and slammed again, and again, and again. I went to work diligently on my pole plant.

Planting the ski poles serves one very important purpose in any type of skiing. Quite simply, when you touch the pole to the snow, that pole provides another point of contact with ground zero. For example, stand on one foot and attempt a few knee bends on that leg. You'll notice you really have to concentrate to maintain your balance on that foot. Now perform the knee bends with one hand on a chair and notice how much easier it is to balance. This is the same type of stabilizing effect a good pole plant has on your balance while skiing. The touch of the pole to the snow lends stability and enhances balance during the transition from turn to turn. However, if the movements you use to plant the poles make you look like you're swatting at flies, you're making it difficult to balance on those skis.

On easier slopes, the importance of the pole plant is less important than on steep slopes. On flatter slopes, however, it remains critical to maintain good hand and arm position. Remember, in these conditions, you're building the habits that will be subconscious reactions in tougher skiing situations, so look sharp! Practice doesn't necessarily make perfect — perfect practice makes perfect.

It is in steep, bumpy, and challenging conditions that the pole plant is absolutely essential. Just try skiing without your poles through the moguls or on a steep slope, and you'll see what I mean. That touch of the pole in these conditions stabilizes the body and provides a pivot point for the lower body to guide the skis about.

So let's plant the poles a few thousand times and learn how to make a good pole plant. In this exercise, start out in a traverse across the hill and as you do, plant both poles over and over by simply swinging the tips forward and touching them to the snow. Remember to keep your hands in a home base

INTERMEDIATE DOWNHILL SKIING

position for balance similar to balancing on the beam, and swing the pole tip forward using only your wrist and forearm.

It's important to simplify the movements you use to swing the pole. You don't want to develop pole plant movements that disrupt your balancing movements. Keep your hands in front and held well away from your body, and simply swing the tip of the pole forward and into the snow.

Getting familiar with the exercise, now perform a few turns and as you do so, keep swinging those poles. As you link turns together, try to start each turn by touching both pole tips to the snow, then beginning the turn. Try to develop the timing by saying to yourself, "touch..., and turn..., touch, and turn." Gary Berger, former technical director of the ski school at Mammoth Mountain used to use this exercise for training ski instructors. It really works and it's a great exercise to use to warm up.

This is an effective exercise for both developing the pole plant timing and good hand positioning, as well as the movement of the pole swing. Practice a few runs making turns and planting both poles over and over. As you get comfortable with the exercise, begin to tighten the rhythm of your turns so you are making tighter turns in the fall line. Now just plant the poles at the start of each turn. Let the touch of the pole plant be the signal to begin the new turn. Keep planting both poles to start your turns so you're solidifying good hand position habits, then gradually work to only planting the downhill pole.

Another exercise that's sort of a spin-off of this one is performed by dragging both poles in the snow as you link turns. You simply lower your stance a bit, and really drag those pole tips, particularly the outside pole tip. The value of this exercise is that the task of dragging the poles aligns the upper body quite nicely over the outside ski. It also develops the habit of keeping the hands and arms in a good position for balance.

These two exercises will work quite well for you if you practice them enough. Again, the best way to use any of the exercises presented in this book are to ski them in a warm up mode. Make your first few runs of any day on smooth, easy slopes working through any of the exercises. Not only will you learn how to better your skiing, but your skiing on that day will be more enjoyable.

Well, now that we have screwed up your entire body with all these weird exercises and drills, let's take your newfound skills and technique and try to apply it to the mountain.

THE UPPER BODY'S CONTROL

Here we go...more drills. This one is done by dragging <u>both</u> poles in the snow, throughout the turns. It's great for getting the upper body in position to effectively plant the poles.

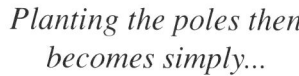

Planting the poles then becomes simply...

Intermediate Downhill Skiing

TOUCH...

...AND TURN

THE UPPER BODY'S CONTROL

TOUCH...

...AND TURN

INTERMEDIATE DOWNHILL SKIING

At this point, you should have a good idea of some of the fundamentals of good skiing, so let's take a few runs at my home base, Mammoth Mountain, and figure out how to apply all this stuff. One thing about Mammoth that makes it so appealing to good skiers is the variety of terrain and snow conditions. On any given day you can find every conceivable type of snow or terrain imaginable.

For this reason we'll use a typical run down from the top of the mountain off the gondola as the route for our private lesson. In the process we'll go through just about everything, from steep to flat, and talk about how and what to apply to the situations we encounter. So cinch those boot buckles down, cause we're starting at the top!

Up here, it's steep and the snow is that classic billiard table smooth packed powder. I don't want to scare you, but here our priority is definitely speed control! In steep slopes, particularly with firm packed snow, there is no room for error, and every turn must serve to keep your speed where you feel comfortable.

With this in mind, priority numero uno is to complete every turn. And do it rather quickly! The more time you spend completing a turn, the faster you go. Remember what we discussed about blending the tipping and twisting efforts in your lower body? Well up here you must get those skis across the hill quickly. This means that as you start the turn, keep the skis flat to the snow and twist them down and across the hill with your feet and legs.

As you twist the skis across the hill to finish the turn, align your upper body over your outside ski so that the ski's edge will bite into the snow and control your speed. Be careful not to try to push the ski into the snow before the skis are across the hill, or you'll start rocketing down the hill with too much speed.

Another priority up here, as far as your technique goes, is to finish every turn with a pole plant. The timing of your pole plant is critical up here, so don't wait until the end of the turn to start swinging the pole tip forward. The pole tip must be planted in the snow at the same time you set the edges to finish the turn, so start swinging the pole forward as the skis are coming across the fall line.

Now, plant the pole and move over your feet again so you can start turning the skis down the hill for the next turn. Try to link five or ten good turns at a

THE UPPER BODY'S CONTROL

Nowhere is the pole plant more important to good skiing than in steep, varying terrain and snow.

time rather than tackling the whole run at first. As you get more familiar with the terrain, direct your vision down the mountain, as opposed to across the mountain. This will tend to keep your body directed downhill and make it easier to link your turns. Okay, now ski the rest of the run and let's re-group down there where the snow gets a bit deeper.

Well, now that we've negotiated the steep and smooth, let's try some of this deep stuff. You're going to need to do things a bit different to effectively ski deep snow, although some of what you just did still applies. The timing of your pole plant is the same. You still keep your vision directed down the hill as you did on the steep packed run. However, now that the snow is deep, it will slow you down some. Let it! Here in the deep, we don't need to be so concerned with getting the skis so far across the hill. In fact, doing so will make it much more difficult to link turns.

So, let's start out easy and try linking about ten turns in this deep stuff. Something I want you to keep in mind is to establish a rhythm to your turns. Rhythm is an aid in skiing deep snow, as it helps to keep your movements flowing and linked together. Try to keep the rhythm with the planting of the pole; "PLANT.., 2.., 3.., PLANT.., 2.., 3..." Doing so will not only maintain rhythm and flow to your turns, but it will also ensure that you keep those pole plants coming.

One more thing before you rip this stuff; keep that inside ski in the snow and get rid of that nasty habit of lifting it to start your turns. When the inside ski is left to just come along for the ride, in deep snow it can get knocked all over the place, in turn knocking you all over the place. Take charge of that thing and guide the inside ski just like you do with your outside ski. Keep it on the snow, and twist that inside foot so the inside ski remains parallel with the outside ski throughout your turns. Okay, give it a try...

Well, frankly, you stunk! Don't worry, the problem is a common one with most skiers in deep snow. You were having some trouble turning those babies with all that snow around your skis — see it all the time. Try it again, but this time put a bit more movement into it. Quite simply, start every turn by jumping up to get the skis out of the snow. With the skis up on top of the snow, it's easier to turn and guide them into the new turn. When you get the skis guided to about the fall line, begin to settle softly back into the snow. Remember that the depth of the snow will slow you down, so you don't need to jump on the skis like on hard snow.

THE UPPER BODY'S CONTROL

As you get more comfortable with the timing and coordination of this movement, you can start to tone down the intensity. At first, the up movement should be rather explosive to get the skis out of the snow. But as you become more confident, smooth this movement so it is a relaxed rising and movement of your body toward the next turn. Okay, try it again and let's ski all the way down to those nasty moguls down there.

Moguls, moguls, moguls, they're everywhere! Try as area managers will to groom them off the slopes, the moguls persevere. Why fight it? Moguls can be a blast to ski if you approach them intelligently. And once again, it's not much different from what we did on the steep or deep. The mechanics of what you do remain — you still turn your feet, you still plant your pole, your vision remains directed down the hill.

However, in the moguls you must turn your feet more quickly and more accurately. There are places to turn and places not to turn. You must plant your pole at the end of every turn — no exceptions. Just try skiing a few turns in the moguls without your poles and you'll see what I mean. Your vision also becomes an integral element of technique for mogul skiing. Much more so than any other situation in skiing, in moguls you gotta' know where you're going!

So first off, ski through a few quick turns here on this smooth section of snow, and use your feet to aim the ski tips where you want them to go. Aim them left and right without relying too heavily on tipping the ski's edges into the snow for control. Make sure every turn ends with a pole plant, and get a feel for the tips of the skis being extensions of your feet. Remember that exercise where we sat on the chairlift and swung the tips left and right with our feet and ankles? Now you can put it to use.

Practice this on smooth snow for awhile until you know what you're trying to do, then take it into the bumps. This is where your vision will come into the act. As you stand at the top of your mogul run, look down and take note of the tops of the moguls. Rather than thinking of where to turn your skis or what path to take, try to plant your pole on the top of every mogul.

If you plant your pole in this manner, and use your feet to aim the ski tips around the mogul without edging the skis too strongly, your mogul skiing will be much easier. Free of the preoccupation with where to turn, you will begin to feel your skis flowing with the terrain of the bumps. Rather than laying the edges into the snow, keeping the skis flatter to the snow will en-

Intermediate Downhill Skiing

Good body positioning with vision & pole plant directed down the hill, shown in static...

...and dynamic form.

able you to aim the skis where you want to go. And with your visual focus of where you're planting your ski poles, you will be making good pole plants and skiing an effective route through the bumps without having to think about these elements separately. OK...ski!

My friend, you are now on the road to that elusive status of ski hero. With practice and focus on the fundamental movements you have read in this book, your skiing will improve. Try to balance the type of skiing you do between disciplined, concentrated work on technique and the let-it-all-hang-out, blast off runs from top to bottom. And for goodness sake, folks, keep it simple! Skiing is first and foremost a sport of beauty and simplicity. I remember once when my friend and mentor, Gary Berger, went off after listening to one of my diatribes. "#%$@!, Posekian, this isn't CALCULUS!! You stand in the %$#@ middle of the %$#@ skis, and you go left and right!! Don't make it sound so %$#@! complicated!!" Definitely words to ski by.

CHAPTER 6
BASE CARE AND WAXING

When you want top performance from your skis, you want the bases and edges in top shape. This means you will want to wax them effectively. The better wax companies spend a great deal of time and money developing and testing waxes. This has allowed them to continually improve the durability of the wax, increase the temperature range for which the wax is appropriate, and make longer lasting waxes. Swix, now in its 50th year, is the leader in this field. We appreciate the assistance given in the preparation of this chapter by Harald Bjerke of Swix.

The major obstacle for a skier to overcome is the friction of the snow — the hydrodynamic forces. The ski base and the wax chosen increase the ability of the ski to glide over the snow. The wax should reduce the friction or suction between the ski and the water under the ski. The pressure of the ski on the snow melts the snow so the skier is usually skiing on a thin coat of water. That water is deeper during warm weather and may sometimes be quite deep as the heat has melted the snow even before the skier crosses it.

Waxes composed of larger molecules are harder than those with smaller molecules. The harder waxes will feel dry when applied. The softer waxes will feel tacky. The harder waxes are for colder weather. The softer the wax, the higher the temperature in which it will be used.

The temperature outside will dictate what wax to use. If the temperature is over 34° F (1° Celsius) it will probably be wet. If it is under 25°F (-4° Celsius) it should be dry so a harder wax will work. If it is between these two temperatures try the hand test. Take a handful of snow and squeeze it. If it clumps together in a ball it is wet; if it does not compact and stays loose, it is dry. The wet snow is warmer, the dry snow is colder.

Intermediate Downhill Skiing

A new snowflake

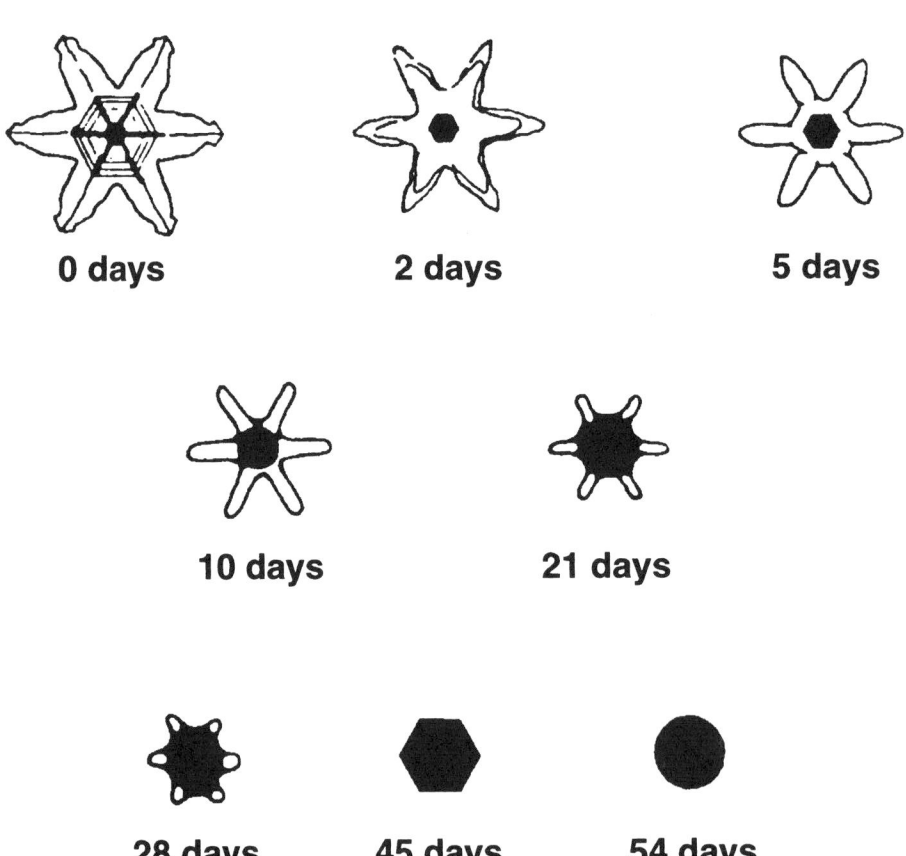

The change of snow crystal at constant temperature and humidity over time.

BASE CARE AND WAXING

Since the water content of snow varies with the altitude and geographical area, the temperature range shown on the wax may not be exact for the snow on which you are skiing. You may have to experiment and move up or down one or two colors to get the perfect wax for your day. So the same temperature in Mammoth, Vail, Chamonix, or Stowe may require quite different waxes to give you equivalent skiing performance. It is best to wax for the coldest snow you expect. The soft wax, used for the warmer snow, will often ice up and stop you from sliding over the snow.

You should do your waxing indoors where the ski and wax are warmer and more workable. The skis must be clean and dry for best results. It is also best to clean your skis indoors. It is preferable to clean the skis after each day's skiing. Do this by taking your plastic scraper and peeling off the excess wax. Then you can use a ski cleaner to finish the job. Always do a good job of cleaning before you put the skis away for the summer.

CHOOSING THE RIGHT WAX

As you become more interested in top performance, you will want to know more of the "whys" and "hows" of waxing. It is a major concern of racers. But even as a beginner you will want to understand why your wax is dragging or is too slippery. Was it your choice of wax or was it your waxing technique? Waxing is both an art and a science. And luck often plays a part too. You may have chosen the perfect wax for the beginning of the day, but then it snowed, or the wind came up, or the sun came out — and your wax was no longer perfect.

You might say that waxing is the mental side of your skiing. It is like chess. You are playing against Mother Nature — and you won't always win.

Humidity is important but only in a general sense. If the humidity is over 50% you can assume that the air temperature is about 4 degrees higher on the Fahrenheit scale (2° Celsius), so you will use a softer wax. If the humidity is over 100%, look up — it's snowing!

Snow granulation varies from the large 6 pointed crystals of newly fallen snow to nearly round crystals of month old snow. For the sharp crystals of new snow you will want a hard wax which will resist the penetration of the snow into the base or the wax. When the snow is warmer and wetter, the wax chosen must have good water repelling properties. It will be a softer wax.

It is much easier to wax for old snow than for new snow. Old snow will have similar characteristics, but new snow varies in terms of dryness, size of flakes, and other characteristics each of which takes a different wax or technique in order to deal with the friction variations. The quality of snow also varies from area to area, so for maximum waxing effectiveness you may have to experiment to find the very best approach to the snow you are skiing.

Heat transfer from the snow relates to both the temperature and the humidity. These factors are, of course, continually changing. If the humidity is high there is more condensation of water on to the snow. A softer wax is therefore required. But if the air is dry, the molecules go from a solid state to gas without first becoming water, so a harder wax than the temperature would indicate should be used.

Wind is another variable in proper wax selection. The wind tends to tighten the smaller snow particles which makes more of the snow come in contact with the ski base. This increases friction. A harder (colder temperature) wax will be used.

Reflection is an often overlooked condition. The snow can absorb energy from the sun, or on cloudy days the heat from the earth can be reflected back by the clouds and absorbed by the snow. In either case there can be a warming. A low angle of the sun or a cover of dry clean snow may result in almost no energy being absorbed by the snow. But a high sun or dirty or wet snow can absorb as much as 65% of the sun's rays.

The resultant snow friction is a combination of the above factors, with temperature being the primary ingredient.

- Wet snow friction occurs when the temperature is above freezing and it is aided by higher humidity or more sun absorption.

- Intermediate snow friction is found when temperatures are 32 to 10 degrees Fahrenheit (0 to -12 C).

- Dry snow friction is found at the colder temperatures (below 10 degrees F or -12 C). It is aided by less humidity, less heat absorption, and more wind.

TOOLS AND ACCESSORIES FOR BASE PREPARATION AND WAXING

Normal preparation is done at the factory. For advanced skiers and racers additional preparation may be desired. If you have a well equipped tool shop you may have most of what you need. If not, here are some of the tools which you may find helpful. We have used the Swix code numbers so that you have

BASE CARE AND WAXING

an idea of what to order. Many of these tools are also available from other manufacturers.

A WAXING TABLE is necessary so that you can work with your skis comfortably. Your own work bench, a high stable table, a Black and Decker bench or the Swix T 76 can all work well.

VISES are required to hold the skis. The Swix T 146X is built especially for skis and has a lip which holds the ski solidly. You should have two such vises. A support vise (Swix T 78) is also desirable to hold up the middle of the ski and reduce the bend.

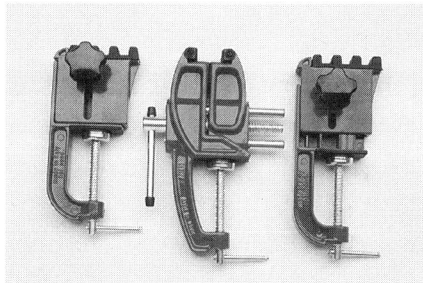

AN IRON, preferably electric, is highly desirable. Any old iron will do, but there are special irons made particularly for skis. The Swix T 7311 or T 7322 can easily select the proper temperatures for efficient waxing. If you are using an old clothes iron, be certain that it is not too hot. If the wax smokes, the iron is too hot. Turn the gauge down until there is no smoking.

SAFETY PRECAUTIONS

Most waxes, Swix included, are quite safe to work with as long as they are not exposed to an open flame and you are not using power tools which will create a dust which can be inhaled. Smaller wax companies may not have the testing potentials of the larger companies and may also use a lower grade of fluorocarbon wax. Check the package to make certain that you have read the required precautionary warnings and the guidelines for application.

When environmentally conscious skiers see the word fluorocarbon they generally think of the chlorofluorocarbon (CFC) gases which pollute the atmosphere. However tests show that the fluorocarbons in the waxes are inert and pose no threat to the environment. For your safety, consider these precautions when waxing:

1. Work in a well ventilated area. You must have a fresh air supply and there should be exhaust fans to evacuate the gases from the waxes.

2. Keep waxes away from open flames such as waxing torches, space heaters, and heat guns. Also, don't smoke while waxing skis. While all waxes can pose a danger, fluorocarbon waxes call for special precautions. At temperatures over 570 degrees Fahrenheit, or 300 Celsius, fluorocarbons disintegrate and become highly poisonous gases. Normal ironing of the waxes does not create this much heat.

3. If you use power brushes to brush on your wax, small wax particles (wax dust) can occur. To reduce this danger, use a paper mask such as is used when working with wood.

4. Use safety glasses when power brushing.

5. Be aware of the flammable character of the solvents you use to clean. Dispose of the rags or Fiberlene (solvent treated paper-like toweling) promptly.

BASE CARE AND WAXING

A RILLER, for base preparation, is used to prepare ski bases for waxing. A rill is a long valley. The riller makes long grooves in your ski bases. If you are not too professional, you can use the edge of a file to rill your bases, but you will get much better results with a professional tool. These tools generally come in several gauges. For alpine skiing usually the Swix T-180 is enough. It has one set of teeth which are .75mm and another which are .5mm. Rilling will be covered more in-depth later in the chapter.

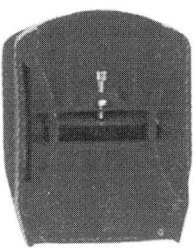

SCRAPERS are made of plastic or metal and are used to smooth the base.

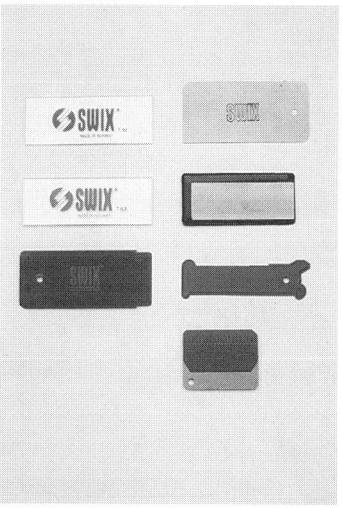

NYLON ABRASIVE PADS, such as Swix Fibertex or Scotch-Brite, are used to remove burrs created by rilling.

SAND PAPER in grades from 320 (very fine) to 100 (most commonly used) to 60 (course) for wet snow.

BASE CLEANER can be any of the traditional solvents and wax removers. These are usually made from petroleum products. Swix has a citrus based cleaner which is more environmentally sound. But since some people are allergic to citrus products, rubber or plastic gloves should be used.

Intermediate Downhill Skiing

SOLVENT IMPREGNATED TOWELS, such as Swix Fiberlene, are very handy for assisting in cleaning the ski bases.

WAX BRUSHES come in many varieties to aid you:

- Stiff horsehair brush (T157) used by racers. Spreads wax and removes excess.
- Hard bristle nylon brush (such as Swix T161) for initial brushing of waxes.
- Soft bristle nylon brush (T160) for final brushing of wax.
- Mixed fiber brush (T155) for removal of all waxes. Especially good for harder waxes.

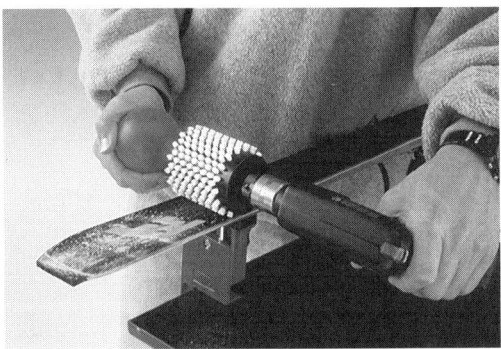

A flat **CORK** (T20) hand piece is used for rubbing in the wax.

BASE CARE AND WAXING

PREPARING THE BASE STRUCTURE OF YOUR SKIS

Factories finish alpine skis by stone grinding or belt sanding. These are generally quite adequate for most snow conditions. However, if you are a racer, or otherwise want the ultimate in performance, you may want a specific base structure for your skis. A specialty tuning shop can provide what you need. But if you are a true aficionado you may want to do it yourself.

In order to improve glide you may want linear textures on the base of your skis. This will allow less of the base of the ski to come in contact with the snow and it will reduce the surface tension of the water under the ski.

Serious skiers will usually rill their bases. Rilling sets grooves into the bottom of the bases which helps to reduce the suction of the water which is formed under the ski when the pressure of the ski melts the snow under it. Those skiing on wet snow are most likely to profit by rilling the skis in order to get the maximum glide.

Bases in need of a new or an improved structure include those which are:

- Very shiny,
- Have a sealed surface from high heat or high pressure base finishing at the factory,
- Have oxidized or dry bases caused by excessive exposure to the elements without being protected by wax.

The type of "structure" desired varies with the amount of friction which the snow will produce. This is dependent on how much water will be under the ski as the ski passes over it. Dry snow will have only the water which is caused by the pressure of the ski. Wet snow will already have a good deal of water which will be increased as the pressure of the ski compresses it. The wet snow creates more suction and increases the drag of the snow.

- For dry snow (5 degrees F, -15 C or colder) you will want a fine structure (shallow rills).
- For intermediate snow friction (5 to 32 degrees F, 0 to -15 C) you will want a medium structure (moderate rills).
- For wet snow (32 degrees F or 0 C or warmer) you will want a

course structure (deeper grooves to allow the water to flow more easily).

Professional preparation is usually your best bet. Let a ski technician structure your skis at the beginning of the season and during the season as the snow conditions change. The technician will generally use machines such as belt sanders or grinders.

INTERMEDIATE DOWNHILL SKIING

Do-it-yourself base preparation can vary from the simple to the complex. The simplest method for producing a fine base for dryer snow is using a #100 sandpaper. Swix silicone carbide sandpaper is very high quality. Use a sanding block or wrap the paper around a file. Sand from tip to tail. The number of passes from tip to tail depends on the amount of texture desired. (If you want an even finer structure because of new snow which is cold and dry, a #150 to #180 grit paper is a good choice.)

For a medium base primarily used for speed events in racing, or to renew a base which has been oxidized, use a wire brush such as the Swix T 163. The bristles should be sharp. Again, brush tip to tail in a single pass.

Choose the proper depth of the rills (grooves) you want on your skis — either .5mm for drier snow, or .75mm. for very wet snow. Support the entire length of the ski with a profile type vise such as the Swix T79.

With a constant pressure, rill the ski from tip to tail using a firm and constant pressure. You can use a single structure (depth of grooves) or you can use a combination of deep and shallow structures. After rilling the base, use a scraper to remove the parts of the base which have been lifted by the rilling.

Whether you sand or brush or rill, you will have raised microfibers from the base which will slow you down if they are not removed. Use Swix Fibertex (T265) or a similar substance to remove these burrs and any remaining oxidized areas of the bases. You can rub the Fibertex in both directions to remove all burrs. There should be no dust remaining. Any micro-fibers or hairs left on the base will limit its gliding potential. You should work the Fibertex both up and down the ski so that no fibers remain. You can then finish with a softer abrasive, such as Swix Fibertex (T266), moving only in the tip to tail direction.

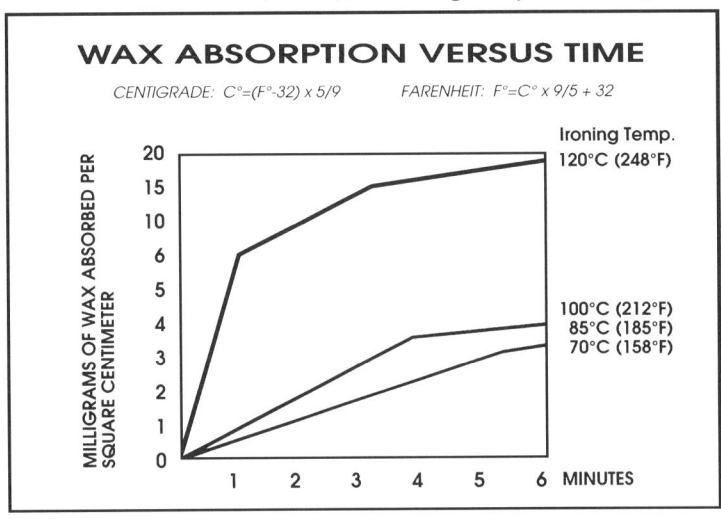

WAX HARDNESS AND COLOR CODING

Each wax is recommended for certain temperature ranges and snow conditions. The warmer colors (yellow and red) are for warmer temperatures. Purple, the combination of red and blue, is next. The blues are colder, the greens for still colder temperatures. The following list includes color waxes from several manufacturers but will give you an idea of what is available.

GREEN is the hardest wax (23 to 3 degrees F, -5 to -18 C). It is for very cold conditions and new or fine grained snow. If this wax is to be used in the warmer range of the recommended temperatures (near 3 degrees F or -16 C) the humidity should be low.

BLUE is a slightly softer wax. The recommended temperatures are 21° to 30° F (-1 to -6 C). If the humidity is higher than 80%, if it is snowing, or if the snow is older, it can be used at temperatures several degrees lower than those recommended.

VIOLET is softer still and is recommended for 30 to 32 degrees F (0 to -1 C). It can be used down to 25 degrees F (-4 C) if the humidity is high or snow is falling.

PINK is often used as a base coat. As a final wax it is best in the 34° to 21° F range (+1 to -6 C)

RED is just a bit softer than the violet. Its recommended temperature range is 32° to 34° F (0 to +1 C). While its primary function is to be effective just above freezing, it will work well a few degrees lower without icing up.

WHITE is the softest wax. It is often made of a silicon formula. The temperature range is 36° to 59° F (+2° to +15° C).

The above list is not all encompassing. For example, Swix makes four graphite waxes for use in low humidity situations. The color codes for the graphite waxes do not match the above temperatures for the same colors.

Preparing to wax:

It is a good idea to use a base wax to make the other waxes last longer. If you are going to do this:

1. Sand lengthwise, tip to tail, with #100 sandpaper.
2. Remove any fibers with Fibertex or a plexi-scraper.

If you have applied a new base structure, you have already done steps 1 and 2.

3. Iron in a thin layer of wax. Let it cool.

4. Apply 2 or 3 additional thin layers, and cork each one smooth. A Swix CH 10 works well for this procedure.

Preparing a new ski:

1. Melt in a sealer wax and polish or cork it in. This will increase the life of the base and give a better surface for other waxes to adhere to.
2. If the base is a bit rough, as is sometimes true for polyethylene bases, a paraffin coat can seal it effectively. (See points 1 to 4 below.)

Often after you have used a ski on hard snow you will have damaged the base. This is called "base burn." While it looks smooth, it actually is quite rough--microscopically speaking. Base burned skis and oxidized bases require this same type of preparation before waxing.

For maximum efficiency the ski bottoms should be treated especially for the use for which they are intended — ice, warm snow, etc. In 1993 the Norwegian wax coach had 70 different ways to prepare ski bottoms. Now he uses only 3. One for wet snow, over 1 degree Celsius; one type for snow that is exactly at freezing; and another for dry snow, below freezing. We may be getting too technical at every level!

Preparing an older ski for a "max-wax" job:

1. Scrape off old wax with a base scraper and with a groove scraper.
2. Brush with a hard brush, then a softer brush — brush from tip to tail.
3. Repair any damaged spots by using a polyethylene stick (such as Swix Polystick T170). From the burning stick drop as much hot polyethylene as needed into the damaged area. After allowing it to cool, scrape off the excess with a steel scraper, a body file (T108). Sand with #220 sandpaper.
4. Smooth the side edges with a steel scraper.
5. If new structuring is required, restructure the base as directed earlier.
6. Scrape the ski base with a razorblade scraper to remove any excess left from the new structuring.
7. Fibertex the ski base to remove excess fibers, dust, and oxidation.

Waxing for a recreational day:

1. Clean the base.
2. Choose the proper wax or waxes.
3. Rub on the wax. Then using a cork, rub it in and smooth it on or iron it on. If you iron it on, you can cork it or scrape it and brush it.

BASE CARE AND WAXING

Waxing for racing:

1. Clean the base. Coat with a soft hot wax (CH8 or CH10) and scrape immediately.
2. After the wax has cooled, brush away the excess wax with a hard bristle brush.
3. Choose the proper wax, apply and iron. Let it cool. Ironing again in about 20 minutes will increase the durability of the wax.
4. If hard waxes (cold temperature) are used, scrape away the thick layer while the wax is still in a semi-soft state.
5. Scrape the groove, the sidewalls, and the edges. Clean the sidewalls with Fibertex.
6. Scrape with a sharp flexible scraper (Swix 823).
7. Brush wax. For harder waxes use a mixed fiber brush (T155), softer waxes a stiff nylon brush (T161).
8. Scrape lightly with the Plexi Scraper.
9. Repeat step 7, then brush.

Between races you may want to use an F4 paste wax. Squeeze a little onto a horse hair brush, then brush the base with a thin coat. The wax should dry quickly.

CARE OF THE EDGES

New skis have edges appropriate to the manufacturers' specifications, but you may want to change them. The 90 degree edges, common on most skis, may be "de-tuned," that is, rounded a bit on the front and back ends to make turning easier. There is no hard and fast rule for this. It is a matter of individual preference.

If you want to care for your own edges and do your own de-tuning you should have the proper tools. An abrasive stone (such as Swix T991), an appropriate file (T106 chrome file), and file guides (Swix T219 through T223). These file guides allow you to file the desired length of the edge with the exact amount of taper (angle) you want. The base edges are controlled with based edge bevel sleeves (T133 with angles of 0, 1, 1.5, and 3 degrees) while the side edges are controlled with side edge bevel sleeves (T117 with angles of 0, 1, 1.5, and 3 degrees).

The base edge should be even with the base or have a slight bevel upward from the base. The ideal bevel angle varies from 0 degrees (a 90 degree corner angle) to 4 degrees for aggressive turning in icy conditions.

INTERMEDIATE DOWNHILL SKIING

Filing the edges is often necessary to remove rust and to smooth out rough spots caused by hitting rocks. Use the same file guides to make certain that the edge stays at the angle you want. Using an unguided file can give you variations in the critical angle of the edge.

If you have hit rocks, sometimes there is a "case hardening" effect — the heat generated by the impact can make the steel extra hard. (You have undoubtedly noted "case hardened" steel on the best tools.) To file this extra hard steel you will need a coarse diamond stone (T236) or another such whetstone. Remove the case hardened areas while using a file guide to keep the proper angle.

Polishing the edges with a fine diamond stone (T235) is important for top level racers. This removes the burrs and polishes away the striations left from the filing.

FOR RACERS AND ADVANCED SKIERS

A more concrete example of the number of Swix "Cera" waxes available to you can be shown in the following chart. There are four levels of categories for their waxes. The color codes are the same for categories 2, 3, and 4 but their uses vary depending on the conditions.

SWIX ALPINE WAXES
Category 1

FC are pure fluorocarbon paste waxes or wax powders. These are the closest waxes to being a universal "one wax fits all" wax. Their temperature range is exceptionally wide.

Cera FC200 is a high level racing wax for temperatures from +15 to -4 degrees Celsius (25° to 60° F) -- Cera FC 100 is for colder conditions 0° to -15° C (32° to 5° F)

Category 2

HF (high fluorocarbon) waxes for fast acceleration, wide temperature range, used for high humidity or wet conditions. Generally used with a category 1 (Cera F) wax as an overlayer.

HF 4 Blue
- 10° to -30° C (-25° to 14° F)
- High humidity, over 80% with very cold temperature
- No need to use an overlayer

HF 6 Violet
- -4° to -10° C (+14° to +25° F)
- Abrasive man-made snow
- Use FC100 as an overlayer

HF 8 Pink
- -6° to +1° C (+21° to +34° F)
- Use as an "iron on" base coat
- Use overlayer of FC100 or 200 (depending on the temperature)

HF 10 Yellow
- 0° to +10° C (+32° to +50° F)
- For very wet conditions (falling wet snow, rain, wet surface snow)
- Use with FC200 as an overlayer
- Dirt in the snow in this temperature range can damage bases, so wax effectively.

Category 3

LF (low fluorocarbon) Used with low humidity, dry conditions.

LF 4 Blue
- -10° to -32° C (-25° to +14° F)
- Use with very cold temperatures and/or harsh man made snow.
- No need for an overlayer unless humidity is higher or the temperature range is at the high end, then use an overlayer of FC100.

LF 6 Violet
- -10° to -4° C (+14° to +25° F)
- Can be used alone or as a base coat for other waxes

LF 8 Pink
- -6° to +1° C (+21° to +34° F)
- For racing use a category 1 FC wax (depending on the temperature) as an overlayer

LF 10 Yellow
- 0° to +10° C (32° to 50° F)
- Because snow may be dirty an overlayer of FC 200 is recommended
- Can be used as a base protecting wax when storing or traveling to avoid oxidation

Category 4

Hydrocarbon waxes with no fluorocarbon additives. These are more economical and more often used by recreational skiers.

INTERMEDIATE DOWNHILL SKIING

CH 4 Ice blue
- -32° to -10° C (-25° to 14° F)
- This is the hardest wax of all.
- Can be mixed with other waxes to increase durability on ice and man-made snow.
- Particularly good for slalom and giant slalom races in this temperature range.

CH 6 Violet
- -10° to -4° C (+14° to +25° F)
- Particularly good for summer skiing on glaciers and for man-made snow.

CH 8 Pink
- -6° to +1° C (21° to 34° F)
- Good base preparation wax and travel wax to protect bases from oxidation.

CH 10 Yellow
- 0° to +10° C (32° to 50° F)
- Use FC200 as an overlayer
- For very wet snow
- Good base preparation and travel wax

CH 11 Silicone White
- +2° to +15° C (36° to 59° F)
- Softest of all of the waxes
- Particularly suited for the wetter conditions of coastal mountains where the snow is often wet.
- A good base for Cera F (FC 200) if the snow is clean.

Graphite waxes are a combination of graphite with a high fluorocarbon (HF) or a low fluorocarbon (LF) wax. These waxes are often ideal in low humidity situations (below 50%). They help to reduce the penetration of the sharp snow crystals into the base or the wax.

HFG 8 (High fluorocarbon graphite) Black
- -6° to +1° C (21° to 34° F)
- Used with "dry glaze" conditions -- low humidity, high sun radiation (new snow and warmer temperatures, such as may occur at higher elevations later in the year.
- Generally mixed with non-graphite wax.
- It is HF 8 with graphite.

LFG 4 (Low fluorocarbon graphite) Blue
- -32° to -10° C (-25° to +14° F)

- Very cold, low humidity wax
- Often used as a base wax for other waxes
- Seldom use an overcoat of category 1 wax with this wax.
- Particularly good for slalom and giant slalom for very icy conditions, even at warm temperatures.

LFG 6 Violet
- -10° to -4° C (14° to 25° F)
- Low humidity counterpart for HF 6 or LF 6
- Good base layer for another race wax
- Often used without an overcoat of category 1 wax

LFG 8 Pink (warm graphite)
- -6° to +1° C (21° to 34° F)
- Low humidity counterpart to HF 8 and LF 8
- Usually used with other waxes
- Use category 1 wax as an overcoat

CHAPTER 7
CONDITIONING

You may have noticed that skiing requires several different types of conditioning. You will need endurance training to make your cardio-respiratory (heart-lung-blood) system work efficiently. You will need endurance in the individual muscles, particularly the abdominals, the upper back and arms, and the thighs. You will need some strength to push yourself with your poles, to maintain your balance and to make your turns — particularly if you are going mogul hopping. You should have a certain amount of flexibility in your joints so that your joints can easily go through a full range of motion. And you must have agility and balance to be able to link turns quickly in steep, bumpy conditions.

CONDITIONING FOR CARDIORESPIRATORY ENDURANCE

Making a long aggressive run down the mountain requires a well-conditioned athlete in terms of cardiopulmonary endurance. The sport is therefore an ideal activity for those who want to feel fit, extend their lives, reduce heart disease and cancer risks, control their weight, and generally feel better. The benefits, of course, depend on how well trained the skier is. For someone who skis several times a week the benefits are very good. For the weekend skier, additional aerobic work must be done off the snow.

If you can ski every day — great! If not, you should look to other forms of endurance exercise, such as running, swimming, or cycling to maintain your aerobic fitness. As your body exercises aerobically (using oxygen which you have inhaled since you started the exercise) you begin to get positive changes in your blood. This begins about 40 seconds after you begin to exercise. Before you have exercised for 40 seconds your body is using anaerobic energy — oxygen which is stored in the muscles or circulating in the blood.

INTERMEDIATE DOWNHILL SKIING

Once you reach the aerobic level, several changes begin to occur. More red blood cells are activated. These are the cells that carry oxygen from the lungs to the muscles and carbon dioxide from the muscles to the lungs to be exhaled. Under the demands of exercise more blood from other organs can flow into the circulatory system. After you have exercised, many of these red cells will remain in circulation. In a few days, however, a large number will go back to the storage organs. But if you do endurance exercise daily you will keep most of the red cells circulating. Your body will then recognize that it needs more red cells so it will create more — if you have sufficient protein, iron, copper, vitamin B_{12}, and the other ingredients necessary to manufacture the cells.

If you were to have a doctor take a red blood cell count before you began an exercise program, then take another sample after you had exercised effectively for an hour, you would find your red cell count increased. Since you have more red cells circulating in your blood, each teaspoon of blood will be able to carry more oxygen to the muscles and more carbon dioxide away from them.

Very simply stated this is how you provide fuel to your muscles:

- Oxygen, from the air which is breathed in, is attracted to the blood cells by the hemoglobin;

- Simple sugars, the simplest usable form of the food you have consumed, are added to the blood;

- From the atoms in these substances the body's own energy sources are rebuilt;

- What remains is carbon dioxide and water. The carbon dioxide is then exhaled.

Obviously the more red cells you have the more efficiently you can transport oxygen to the muscles and carbon dioxide away from them. This becomes even more important when you move to higher altitudes. At sea level nearly 21% of air is oxygen. Almost 79% is nitrogen. When you exhale almost 16% of your exhaled air is oxygen and about 3 1/2% is carbon dioxide.

If you were go to an altitude of 10,000 feet (3050 meters) the amount of available oxygen drops about 30%. To make up for this oxygen lack you will breathe more often and as you become acclimated to the altitude, in about a week, your red blood cells will have increased. Still, the amount of oxygen in your blood will have dropped by about 8%. When you come back to a lower altitude you will have more endurance for several days because the increased number of red cells will stay with you for a while. This is why endurance athletes such as cross country skiers, marathon runners, and swimmers often train at higher altitudes.

If you have trained effectively aerobically at the lower elevations by doing aerobic dance, running, swimming, cycling, or long distance skating, your red cells will have already increased and you will be ready for exercise at the higher elevation.

To improve your endurance you must increase your heart rate significantly for at least 20 to 30 minutes. This is long enough to give you the necessary benefits to reduce heart attack risk. But if you are training for 6 to 8 hours on the mountain you will profit by longer workouts.

How much cardiorespiratory fitness you need is dependent on how and where you will ski. If you can walk out of your front door and put on your skis and merely want a couple of slides down the hill forget this program and just lace up your boots whenever you are ready. But if you want to go hard through the moguls, take a run from the top to the bottom, or you're going to a much higher altitude to ski, you are well advised to begin a conditioning program before your trip.

It is wise to work out at least three days a week for six weeks. Six days a week is better but, of course, anything is better than nothing.

The generally accepted standard for endurance exercise is to get your heart rate to an acceptable level for 20 to 30 minutes. That "acceptable" level is 65 to 85% of your maximum heart rate. Your maximum heart rate is considered to be 220 heart beats per minute less your age. So if you are 20 years old it would be 220 minus 20 which is 200. 200 multiplied by .65 gives you 65% of your maximum heart rate. You then work out with a pulse rate of between 130 and 170 for 20 to 30 minutes. If you are 40 years old the calculations would be 220 - 40 = 180, and 180 x .65, so you would work out with a pulse rate of between 117 and 153. If you are 60 the figures would be 220 - 60 = 160 so your target heart rate would be between 104 and 136.

If you are in average condition your resting pulse rate will be in the 70's. As you get in better shape your resting pulse rate will drop because you will have more red blood cells working for you so your heart doesn't have to beat as often to get its work done. You can tell if you are getting in better condition by measuring your resting pulse rate. When it drops into the mid-60's you are in better than average condition. When it gets into the 50's you are in pretty good shape. In the 40's you are in great shape. A few world class endurance athletes have pulse rates in the 20's.

To check your pulse you can put your fingers, not the thumb, on the opposite wrist just above the thumb. Or you can put them just below your ear on the inside of the muscle on the side of your neck. Some people just like to put their hands over their hearts and feel the beat. Once you feel the beat count the number of beats in a minute. This is your pulse rate. Or you can count for 15 seconds and multiply that number by 4 to get the number of beats in a minute. If you are exercising it is often easiest to count the beats for only 6 seconds then multiply that number by 10 to get your pulse rate during exercise.

Before you start an exercise program it is always a good idea to have a physical examination. This will give you your blood pressure, your cholesterol levels, your red blood cell count, the condition of your heart and a number of other important indicators.

Any exercise that gets your heart beating fast enough to get into your target zone is good. Cross country skiing, swimming, running, cycling — even sex. Just remember that whatever you are doing, get to your target rate and stay there for at least 20-30 minutes. Also you should warm up before you hit your target range. So just perform your activity at a little slower pace for a few minutes before you speed up and hit your target rate. Then at the end of your exercise cool down by slowing your exercise and letting your heart rate drop. Then finish with some stretching. Some people like to stretch before their aerobic workout. That's OK. Just do some aerobic warm up, such as jogging or skiing, then stretch, then get into your real aerobic workout. Then stretch again. The stretching after the workout is more important than that done before the workout.

DEVELOPING MUSCULAR ENDURANCE

It's not enough to have your heart healthy and more red blood cells. Your individual muscles also have to have specific endurance. The muscles you use in an endurance activity will develop a better capacity to use the oxygen and sugars which the blood brings to them. There will be more hemoglobin in the muscles, more readily available fuel, and there may even be a different type of muscle tissue developed.

There are three different types of muscle fibers, the slow twitch (red or type I), the intermediate (type IIa), and the fast twitch (white or type IIb). The fast twitch fibers contract quickly but cannot do it for many repetitions. Olympic weight lifters have a high percentage of these because they need only one powerful contraction, then they rest for many minutes. Endurance athletes, such as cross country skiers, swimmers, and distance runners have a large percentage of the slow twitch fibers. These fibers contain more fuel and can contract many times. Alpine skiers are somewhere in between.

Research indicates that the type of training a person does can change the type of fibers present. It may be that it is the intermediate fibers which change more toward the fast or the slow twitch type of fiber. Trained cross country skiers have about 80% of their fibers as slow twitch. It would seem then that appropriate aerobic training should be able to develop more effective muscles and better muscular endurance.

In the off season, the summer and fall, swimming (especially the crawl or the back stroke) will not only help to maintain one's aerobic level in the cardiorespiratory system, but it will develop more of the slow twitch fibers in the upper back (latissimus dorsi) and the back of the arms (triceps). If you're still riding a rope tow these should be a great help. On the other hand skating, running, or cycling should help to develop such muscles in the legs.

For these reasons, many people do cross training in the off season. This may include 2 or 3 days of running, cycling, skating or working on a cross country ski machine (such as Nordic Track) for the lower body and 2 or three days of swimming, rowing or paddling for the upper body.

Another exercise which will condition your legs can be done while you watch TV. Put five or six books on the floor in a stack. Start with both feet on one side of the books then jump to the other side, landing on both feet. Continue to jump back and forth without stopping until tired. Jumping rope is another exercise which will condition both your heart and your legs.

INCREASING YOUR STRENGTH

Muscular endurance and muscular strength are at opposite ends of the spectrum. Strength is how much force can you generate in one muscular contraction while endurance is how long can you continue muscular contractions with relatively little resistance against them. In skiing you never need absolute maximum force as an Olympic weightlifter would need. But there are times when you need more than the normal amount of force, such as when running the gates or popping off moguls — or even when getting up after a fall. So there is a need for more strength at times. And when going up a hill there is a need for more than the average amount of strength for a number of muscular contractions.

Your strength is determined primarily by the number of individual muscle fibers you can have contracting in one contraction. No one can contract all of the muscle fibers in a muscle at the same time. Few people can even contract 50% of their muscle fibers at one time. So your strength training program is designed to teach your brain to be able to contract more muscle fibers at one time.

The following exercises will help you to condition your muscles. If you are trying to get stronger, exhaust your muscles in under ten repetitions. Exhaustion in one to three repetitions is best. But if you are working on developing muscular endurance, such as you will use in making a long run, do a number of repetitions. You will be able to tell whether your are developing your muscular endurance by how your "quads" feel at the end of the day.

25 to 100 repetitions would be a good range for most people. But remember that your muscles should be exhausted when you finish. It is only by getting your muscles very tired that you will get the best results. However, remember that anything is better than nothing.

The strength exercises which will condition you better for skiing are:

THE ABDOMINAL CURL UP. Everyone knows this exercise but some have not kept up with the latest techniques to make it more effective.

- Lie on the floor

- Put your hands on your chest (to avoid pulling in on the neck muscles).

- Bring your feet up as close to your hips as possible (so that you don't use the small hip flexing muscles which attach to the lower back — especially important for women),

- Look at the ceiling and continue looking at the same spot during the exercise (so that you don't stretch the muscles in the back of your neck), then

- Raise your shoulders and concentrate on bringing the lower part of your ribs closer to the top of your hips.

- Do as many repetitions as you can because you want muscular endurance from these muscles.

CONDITIONING

This exercise strengthens the abdominal muscles which will begin your poling action. As you start to pole you will bend forward at the waist. These muscles do that.

There are actually four sets of muscles in the abdominal wall. One, the rectus abdominis, does most of the work in the sit up. There are two sets of angled muscles called the "obliques." These assist in the sit up but also work in twisting and sideward bending actions. The following exercises work on the "obliques."

THE TWISTING ABDOMINAL CURL UP is done the same as the above exercise but as you raise your shoulders you bring your right shoulder toward your left knee on one repetition, then your left shoulder to your right knee on the next one.

If you belong to a gym with a rotary abdominal machine you use it. It is more effective than the twisting sit up.

Another exercise which can develop the abdominal obliques is the side sit up. Put your feet under a sofa or have someone hold them down, then, while on your side bring your shoulders and torso upward.

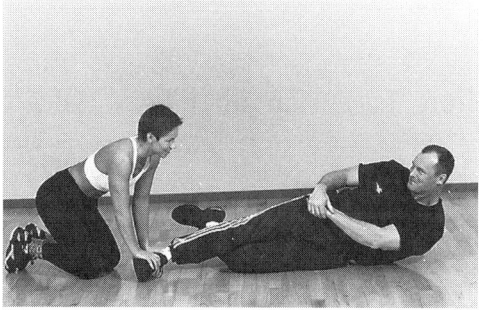

Another particularly good exercise is done lying on the floor on your back. Extend your legs straight over your hips. With your arms out to your side to

INTERMEDIATE DOWNHILL SKIING

keep your torso flat, allow your legs to come down to the right side, then bring them back up, then down to the left side.

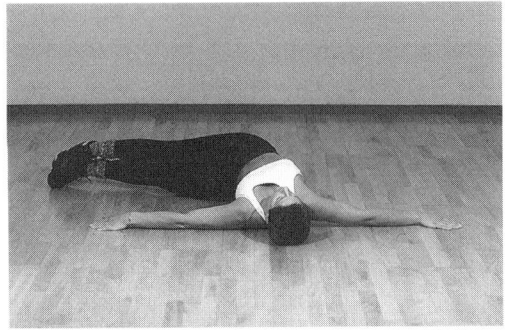 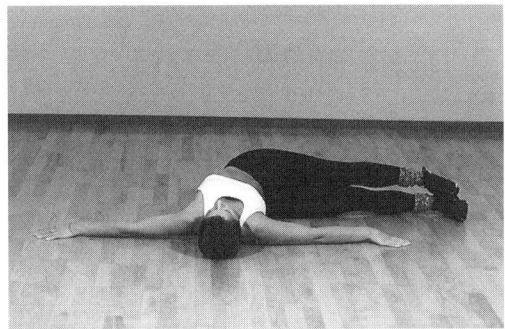

SHOULDER EXTENSION is another important exercise for most people to do unless they have been swimmers or gymnasts. The upper back and back of the arm muscles are not used as often in other sports. It is these muscles, the latissimus dorsi or upper back and the triceps of the rear of the upper arm which stabilize the poles during your pole plant, and do the pushing when you are moving on a flat plane or slightly uphill. Ever notice that after a day of skiing early in the season that the back of your shoulders hurt? This will prevent that.

If you belong to a gym use a pull down pulley and pull it down with your arms straight. If you don't belong to a gym you can buy stretching bands at a sporting goods store or surgical tubing (about 8 to 10 feet) from a pharmacy. Screw an eye bolt into a door jamb or into a wall in the garage, anchor the middle of the band to the bolt. Tie knots in the end of the tubes, or make a handle, then pull — alternating arms or using both arms together. You want to use your muscles through the same range of movement you will use in skiing so pull from a spot directly in front of your shoulders to as far back as you can pull.

Another way to develop these muscles is with a partner skier. Take two lengths of rope at least 6 feet long. Face each other. Each holds one end of each rope.

CONDITIONING

While facing each other each pulls back with their right arms while they resist each other with their left arms. Then they both pull with their left arms while they resist each other with their right arms. Both the pull and the resisting are working the "lats" and one of the three heads of the triceps. While doing this exercise keep the arms straight, no bend at the elbows.

THE TRICEPS (three heads) straighten (extend) the elbow. One of the three heads crosses the shoulder joint so it works with the "lats" in pulling the upper arm backward. All three heads work to straighten the arm at the elbow joint. This is done in the last part of the poling action.

If you belong to a gym use the triceps extension machine or do triceps extensions on the "lat" pull down machine. If you don't belong to a gym you can do push ups with either your feet or your knees on the floor.

Intermediate Downhill Skiing

THE FRONT OF THE THIGH (quadriceps) holds you in that bent leg position which is critical to downhill skiing. There is no question that these are the most important muscles for the alpine skier. You will want both muscular strength and muscular endurance in this group.

If you are in a gym use the quadriceps machine. If not, get a partner. Sit on a table. Have your partner place both hands on your ankle and give resistance. You straighten your leg. If you don't have a partner you can use that same rubber band which was recommended for the upper back.

CONDITIONING

THE BACK OF THE THIGH (hamstrings) must be strong to counterbalance the quadriceps. Gyms have special machines for the hamstrings. If no machine, get your trusty old partner, lie face down on the floor or a table, and have your partner push against your ankle as you lift your lower leg from the floor. Keep the other knee on the floor.

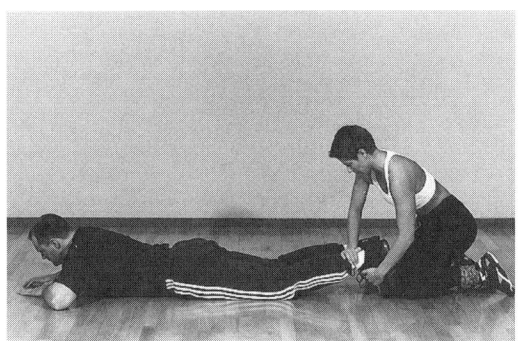

INTERMEDIATE DOWNHILL SKIING

THE BACK OF THE HIPS (gluteals) work with your quads to control your skiing stance. To get the gluts, the muscles that do a lot of your power work, with your quads, lie on a table face down with your hips on the table but your thighs past the table and your toes touching the floor. You can use a partner, if you want more strength, or do it alone, if you want more endurance by doing many repetitions. Start with one toe touching the floor while the other leg is brought as high as possible then alternate legs. This will look like an exaggerated kicking action for a person swimming the crawl stroke.

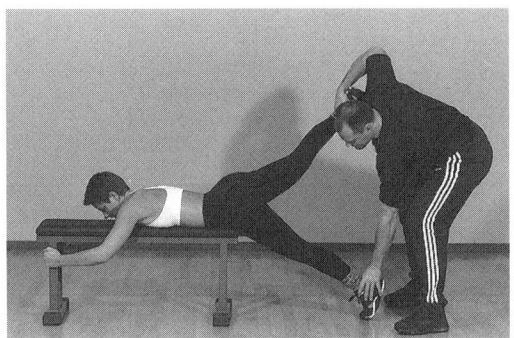
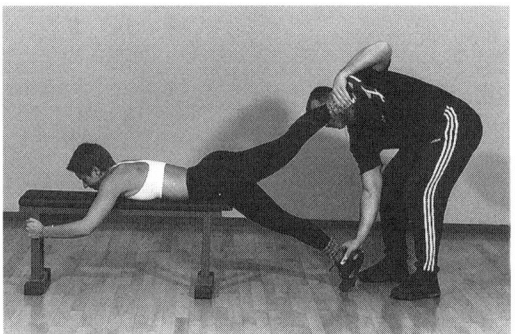

CONDITIONING

HIP AND KNEE EXTENSION gives you greater force potential from your hips and knees. Gyms all have either squat racks, sleds, or other machines which allow you to extend your legs. But it can be done easily at home. You can just do a 3/4 knee bend (don't bend your knees over 90 degrees) or you can do half knee bends. If you want twice the amount of resistance do your knee bends with only one leg. To do a half knee bend, hold a table top to steady yourself. Using only one leg, bend down 45 to 90 degrees then return to a standing position. By doing it on only one leg you get the same effect as doing it with two legs while holding a barbell equal to your own weight.

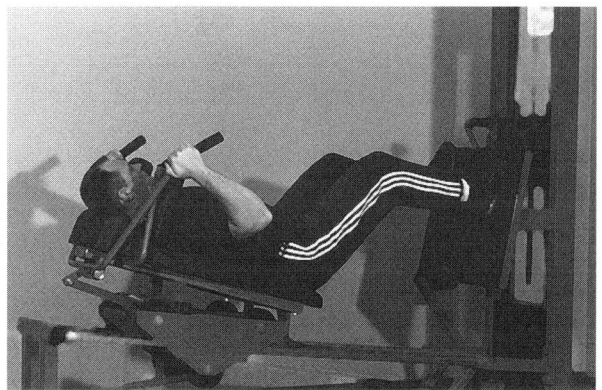

INTERMEDIATE DOWNHILL SKIING

CALF MUSCLES (gastrocnemius) are done by simply rising up on your toes then bringing your heels back to the ground. Repeat many times for endurance. If you want more strength, such as for hill climbing, balance yourself by holding a table or chair then do the exercise using only one leg at a time--the right leg until it is exhausted, then the left leg until it is exhausted.

HIP ABDUCTORS are those which move your legs sideways away from the mid-line of your body. They are very important in helping you to maintain your balance. When you shift your weight to a new uphill ski for turning, it is the adductors, those muscles on the outside of your lower hip, which stop your motion outward and allow you to catch your balance.

Some gyms have special machines for the abductors. If there is a "multi-hip" machine, use it. Most gyms have low pulley weights with ankle straps. Stand with one side of your body next to the machine and put the ankle strap on the leg farthest from the machine. Lift the leg sideways keeping it straight.

With a partner, lie on your side. Let your partner put pressure on your knee or ankle, then lift your leg as high as you can. If you have no partner you can do the same exercise alone — you won't get as strong, but you can get just as much endurance.

You can also use the rubber bands. Attach one to a low part of a wall, hook your foot into a loop on the end of the band, and lift your leg outward.

CONDITIONING

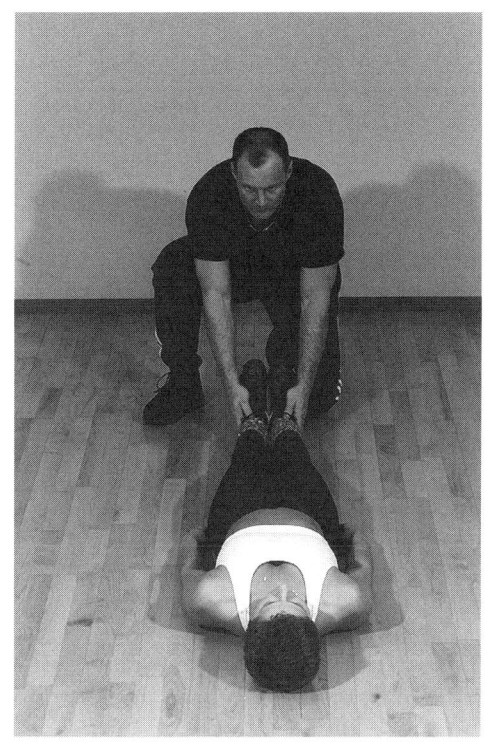

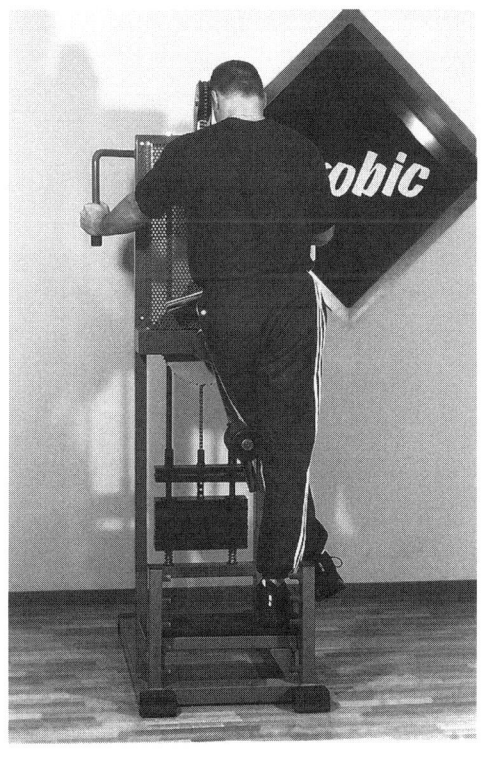
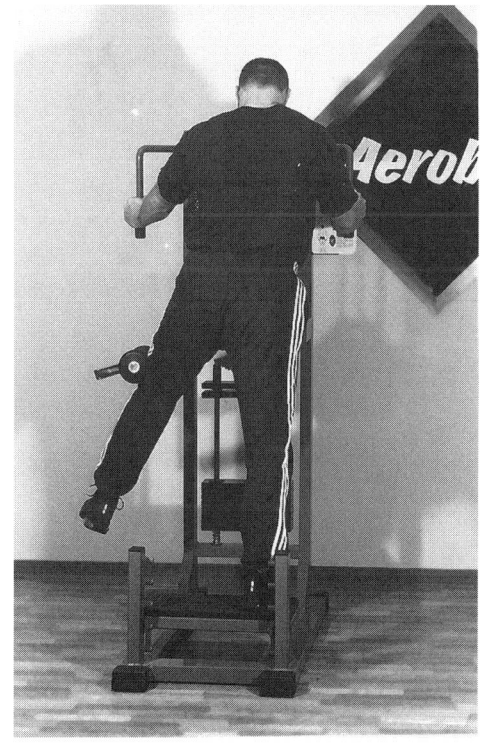

Intermediate Downhill Skiing

HIP ADDUCTORS are those muscles high on the inside of your thighs. They also help in balancing. They also bring your legs back together if they have been moved outward by the abductors. The exercises are just the reverse of those for the abductors.

If your gym has a machine, use it. If there is a low pulley station stand sideways to the pulley but a yard away from the machine. Put the ankle strap on the ankle nearest the machine. Let your leg move outward (toward the machine) with the weight, then bring it back to the other leg.

It can be done with a partner. Lie on your back. Spread your legs. Let your partner give pressure inside your ankles. Bring your legs back together. If you wish, you can combine the adductor and abductor muscles in this exercise. While lying on your back, your partner will give you hand pressure on the outside of both ankles. You will spread your legs against the pressure (abductors). Then your partner will give you pressure on the inside of your ankles and you will bring your legs back together (adductors).

Without a partner just sit on the floor with your feet about 12 inches from your hips and the heels together. Spread your knees outward, then grasp the inside of your knees with your hands. Bring your knees together as you resist the movement with your hands. You will feel the tension inside your upper thighs.

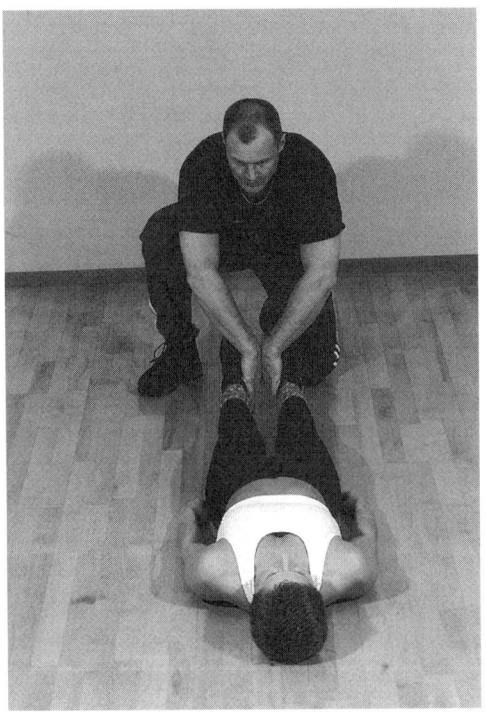 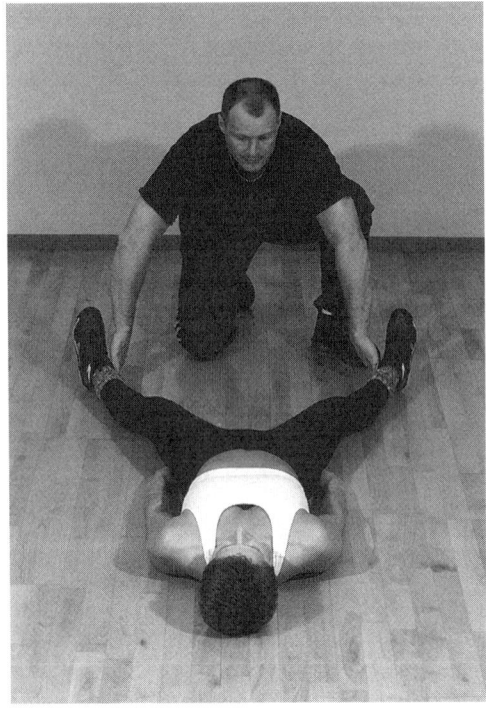

CONDITIONING

 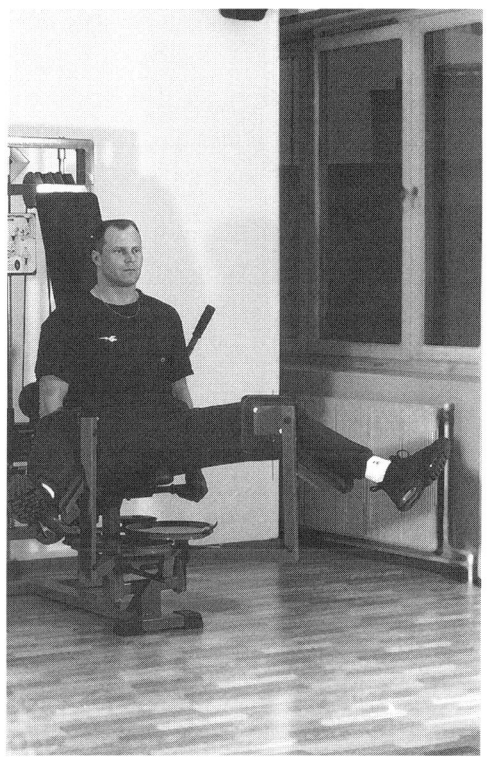

THIGH ROTATION develops the muscles which move your ski tips in or out. This action is done high in the hips. Sit on the floor with your legs stretched out. Turn your feet inward as far as they can go and hold. Then twist outward — and hold. It is more effective if a partner can give your feet resistance in each direction.

Intermediate Downhill Skiing

LOWER BACK exercises should be more geared to muscular endurance than strength so you will want many repetitions. You can lie on the floor face down and lift your shoulders about 6 inches from the floor then return to the floor. (You don't want to go too high with your shoulders because you don't want to create a "sway back" in your exercise.)

You can also do this with a partner. With the partner holding your legs, and your hips and legs on a table, bend forward at the waist to 60 or 90 degrees then lift your torso back up so that it is in line with your legs and hips. Again, you don't want to arch your back during the exercise.

How many repetitions and how much weight you use depends on your goals. For pure strength you should be exhausted in 1 to 3 repetitions. But pure strength is not what you want for skiing. You want a certain amount of strength and you want muscular endurance. So you will want from 20 to over 100 repetitions. But anything you do will help.

Using a partner, or "manual resistance," can actually be better than using weights. Your partner can adjust the pressure to make you work to a maximum level on each repetition. Weights can't do this. Only partners and "isokinetic" machines have this capability. So if you are using a partner, don't think you are not getting the best strength work out. In fact, that partner is probably entitled to a good dinner once a week for helping you to develop your "habit."

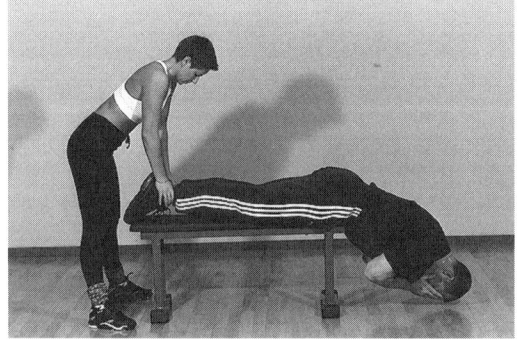
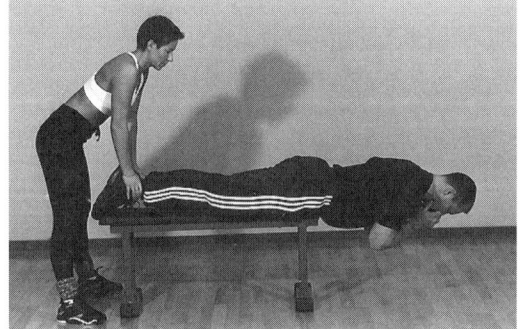

CONDITIONING

BECOMING MORE FLEXIBLE

Flexibility comes from stretching the body's connective tissue: the tissue that holds one bone to another (ligaments), the tissue which holds muscles to bones (tendons), and the tissue which holds the individual muscle bundles together. If you are not flexible you will not have a full range of motion for each joint. When you are too tight you must use excess muscle power just to make a simple movement. If you are not sufficiently flexible it is easier to sprain (ligament damage) or strain (muscular or tendon damage).

Flexibility is quite simple to achieve. Most of us touched our toes every day during physical education classes in school but we may have forgotten to continue the practice. You could probably easily touch your toes when you were 12. Can you do it now? The connective tissue tends to shorten if we do not keep it stretched, so most of us have lost some flexibility between the eighth grade and now.

Stretches should be held for 20 to 30 seconds in order to get the maximum benefits. If you find that you are particularly tight in one area, do the exercise several times a day.

THE TOE TOUCH keeps your lower back and the back of your hips and thighs flexible. While most people do it standing, it is more effective to do it sitting on the floor. When you are sitting and stretching forward, the muscles in the back of your torso and thighs relax so you can stretch farther. When you are standing, those same muscles remain somewhat tight because they are fighting the gravity which is allowing you to bend downward.

INTERMEDIATE DOWNHILL SKIING

ABDOMINAL TWISTING is essential for the downhill skier. The rotation you make with every turn requires a flexibility in this area. With your legs spread about shoulder width, twist as far as you can in one direction. Not too fast! Now hold for 20 to 30 seconds. Then twist the other way.

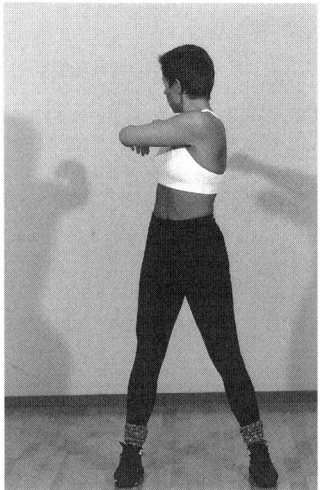

THE UPPER CHEST AND SHOULDER STRETCH is not only good to prevent round shoulders, but it will allow you to be more efficient in your poling action. With your arms at shoulder level, pull them backward as far as they will go — and hold.

THE FRONT OF THE SHOULDER STRETCH also allows you to work your poles better. While standing with your arms at your side, bring both arms directly backwards as far as you can — and hold.

TRAINING FOR AGILITY AND BALANCE

You are already well aware that skiing is a balance sport along with its strength and endurance requirements. Skiing technique is all about balance in motion. Just think about all of the internal and external factors that must be balanced and counterbalanced to move down the mountain continually turning and shifting your balance. You've got the steepness of the slope, the depth and density of the snow, the texture of the snow, the visibility, all of which is varying from turn to turn. And in order to skillfully ski through all this, you've got to be balanced on one ski most of the time. When turning you must guide them left and right in order to regulate your speed and momentum. Indeed, high level skiing requires an unbelievable sense of balance and equilibrium.

You cannot get enough work on balance, on or off the snow. When you balance you are training your brain. It must continually make adjustments in your muscle contractions to keep you from falling right or left, forward or backward. If you are standing on one leg your balance forward and back is pretty easy because your foot is longer than it is wide. If you put on skis this difference is emphasized because the ski is longer than your foot but it is narrower than most feet — and it is more slippery than are your foot bottoms!

So while forward backward balance is essential, it is much easier to achieve than side to side balance. Add to this the fact that while skiing you shift your weight from one ski to the other quickly. If you are standing on a floor on two feet then slowly shift your weight to one foot, it is difficult enough to balance. But when you jump to one foot and try to hold a balanced position before hopping back to the other foot, it is much more difficult. But it is this dynamic shifting of balance thousands of times during a day which is the key to your improved technique.

Olympic skiers practice balance exercises daily. Here are a few exercises to help you with your balance. The first two exercises work on static balance — balance which does not move laterally. The third drill and the skating drills deal with dynamic balance.

ONE LEG BALANCE is a start. Balance on one foot then the other. Hold the balance on each foot as long as possible. Time yourself on how long you can hold each balanced position. The muscles on the inside and the outside of your hips and thighs will both work in this drill. As you start to sway outward the inside muscles contract. As you start to sway inward the outside muscles contract.

BALANCING ON A FLEXED LEG is a bit more difficult. Take your one foot balance position. Slowly lower your hips until your knee is at about a 60 degree angle. Your hips should lower 8 to 10 inches. Move up and down for 15 seconds or until you have lost your balance. Now do it on the other leg. The same muscles work as in the above drill, but because you are moving up and down other muscles come into play and the muscles which hold you balanced must react to different stimuli.

HOPPING BALANCE is a more advanced balance drill. With your weight balanced on one foot, hold for five seconds or until you start to lose your balance then hop sideways to the other foot and hold. Continue hopping from one leg to the other. Learn to hold each new balanced position for 5 seconds. Start with 6 inch hops. Eventually aim for 24 inch hops.

In this drill not only are the balance muscles working, but if you don't hop far enough outward the muscles on the outside of your hips must work to

Intermediate Downhill Skiing

pull you into the proper position. If you shift too much weight outward, the inner thigh muscles must pull you back or you will fall outward. This drill is critical to teaching your brain just how quickly it must shift the body weight and how far it can shift it.

Roller blades or "in line" roller skates will help you with the dynamic balance needed on the snow. Skiing on in-line skates can be quite easy, especially for skilled skiers. Think about it; you don't have seven feet of ski attached to your feet so the skates are quite easy to turn. The pavement is usually smooth and consistent and the whole situation is really quite predictable. Also the skates hold the road easier than skis hold the snow.

If you are comfortable going left and right while skating, start being creative and do some things which will increase your balance on skis. Set up a slalom course. Use rocks or traffic cones or your kids' toys to make a course that you can skate through — just like in the Olympic slalom course. Stagger the "gates," create a course which will challenge your balance — then start skating. Cut left and right, wide turns and sharp turns. Make it fun. It will help you to be a better skater and a better skier.

Another way to develop your skating skills is to play roller hockey. It's a great workout as the spirit of competition motivates you to do some really dumb things. Sprinting for the puck, quick direction changes, and a lot of quick starts and stops are all great for your reactions and coordination. You'll want to wear all the protective garb you can get your hands on, as you may crash occasionally. When you get into it, roller hockey is great for your reactive movements and agility. You'll get in and out of body positions you would never feel going up and down hills. Quite simply, it's a blast and it will pay off great dividends come next season.

Setting gates on a moderately steep road is also a great training aid. It simulates the movements of skiing and can help you to develop an aggressive attitude. Set 'em with lots of turns — short turns, then try to generate speed between the gates. Don't try so much to better your technique. Instead, try to acquire that attitude of aggressively going after the next turn, rather than waiting for it to come to you. If you can do it on skates, you'll be able to do it on skis.

Play on skates while you increase your sense of balance and equilibrium. It's still important to make some turns, but the emphasis should be toward doing things on skates that allow you to move free of the preoccupation of technique. Learn how to move for balance, not for looks! Also, don't worry about strength or endurance or anaerobic capacity, just make it fun. If you put some chutzpah into the games you play on skates, you'll get stronger, you'll last longer, and have more fun in the process. And next ski season, when that snow flies and you're on the boards once again, you'll be ready to rip! But, do watch out for those first couple of turns.

Conditioning effectively helps your body to be the best tool that it can be for effective skiing. It also keeps your physiological age reduced. A well-conditioned 60 year old may have the musculature and heart of a person less than 30. So effective conditioning can make you look and feel better. And certainly it will reduce any unwanted tiredness or soreness on your first run of the winter!